MORE
LATIN AND ENGLISH IDIOM

MORE
LATIN AND ENGLISH IDIOM

AN OBJECT-LESSON FROM
LIVY XXXIV. 1–8

BY

H. DARNLEY NAYLOR, M.A.
Trinity College, Cambridge
Professor of Classics in the University of Adelaide

Cambridge :
at the University Press
1915

CAMBRIDGE
UNIVERSITY PRESS

University Printing House, Cambridge CB2 8BS, United Kingdom

Cambridge University Press is part of the University of Cambridge.

It furthers the University's mission by disseminating knowledge in the pursuit of education, learning and research at the highest international levels of excellence.

www.cambridge.org
Information on this title: www.cambridge.org/9781316619919

© Cambridge University Press 1915

First published 1915
First paperback edition 2016

A catalogue record for this publication is available from the British Library

ISBN 978-1-316-61991-9 Paperback

PREFACE

A KINDLY critic of my *Latin and English Idiom* suggested in *The Classical Review* that I should turn my hand to Cicero. If I have not done that, I have at least turned my hand to Livy as a speech-writer.

These first eight chapters of Book XXXIV are peculiarly fitted for separate treatment. They deal with an episode which stands entirely by itself, and there is no need to wrench the setting in order to obtain the jewel. Then, again, they possess a special interest because in them we have two speeches, one in favour of, the other against a bill before Parliament. Finally Livy gives us a vivid picture of Cato inveighing against the Roman Suffragettes. It may then, perhaps, be said of my work that

> "some modern touches here and there
> Redeem it from the charge of nothingness."

I have to thank for help of various kinds my friends Professor W. Mitchell, M.A., D.Sc., Mr D. H. Hollidge, M.A., and Mr R. J. M. Clucas, B.A.

H. D. N.

ADELAIDE UNIVERSITY,
December, 1914.

INTRODUCTION

THE VALUE OF ANCIENT LANGUAGES AND OF TRANSLATION INTO IDIOMATIC ENGLISH

THE educational value of great ancient languages is enhanced by, if it does not depend on, the fact that such languages differ from our own in methods of thought and expression. Thus comparisons have to be made continually, intelligence is quickened, and powers of observation are developed. That is why French and German (especially the former) can never be adequate substitutes for Latin and Greek.

The purpose of this book, as of my *Latin and English Idiom*, is to encourage detailed comparison of two fine languages. In spite of all that has been urged to the contrary, I am still of the opinion that, except from the few who possess a natural gift of imitation, continuous Latin Prose should not be demanded. In its place we should require a far higher standard of English translation, and should expect a candidate to explain why his English version is often so different in form from that of the original. If we give him Cicero to translate, he should be told to make his version sound like Burke, Bright, or Gladstone; if Livy, to make it sound like Prescott or Froude; and he should be asked, also, to justify any modernizations in which he may have indulged. For modernization or Anglicizing should be encouraged when the learner translates from the foreign language, just as Latinizing and Grecizing are encouraged in the reverse process.

LATIN ORDER

A less kindly critic of my *Latin and English Idiom* has said that I am like one who has just discovered the importance of Latin order. If indeed I have awakened to its importance, I ought to be thankful; for some Homers seem to be napping still. A well-known version of the *Aeneid* translates 7. 312

Flectere si nequeo superos, Acheronta movebo

by "if I cannot bend the gods, I will stir up Acheron." Apart from the unhappy picture which this version calls up—tin gods to bend, and mud to stir up—, can it be said that the magnificent antitheses of *flectere* and *movebo*, of *superos* and *Acheronta* (both crying out for notice because of the order) are represented at all? If distinguished scholars can thus miss the mark, what may we not expect of beginners[1]? I remain, therefore, unrepentant and

[1] I relegate to a footnote two random examples of Conington's indifference to order from Vergil's *Georgicon* Book i.

(1) ll. 297–8

At rubicunda Ceres medio succiditur aestu
Et medio tostas aestu terit area fruges.

On *tostas* C. says "not to be joined with *aestu*." But, unless Latin order is a wild Chinese puzzle, *medio...aestu* must go with *tostas*. The ears, as a matter of fact, *are* parched *by* the midsummer heat, but they are also bruised *in* the midsummer heat (on the threshing-floor). The truth is that the ablative *medio...aestu* is first an instrumental ablative with *tostas* and then a temporal ablative with *terit*.

(2) ll. 316–21

Saepe ego cum flavis messorem induceret arvis
Agricola et fragili iam stringeret hordea culmo,
Omnia ventorum concurrere proelia vidi,
Quae gravidam late segetem ab radicibus imis
Sublimem expulsam eruerent, ita turbine nigro
Ferret hiemps culmumque levem stipulasque volantes.

On l. 319 C. writes: "*late* with *eruerent*." But *late* can only go with *gravidam...segetem*, for it lies between them. Compare Livy 3. 2. 13 multas

repeat that learners should be taught to read Latin with
emphasis on the words abnormally placed; and I venture,
further, to repeat that departure from the normal order is
what makes Latin *visually* so effective an instrument of expression.

English depends on intonation and stress, and the same
words can bear quite different meaning according to the intonation or stress used in uttering them. To take a simple case:
the words "I cannot walk there" may mean, according as we
pronounce them, (1) *I* cannot walk there (but you can);
(2) I *cannot* walk there (if I want to); (3) I cannot *walk*
there (but I can ride); (4) I cannot walk *there* (but I can walk
half the distance). Latin can show all the last three meanings
by order: the first is expressed by inserting *ego*. Thus we get
for (1) ego eo ambulare non possum; (2) non possum eo ambulare;
(3) ambulare eo non possum; (4) eo non possum ambulare.

Often it is order which elucidates the interpretation of some
doubtful word in poetry. Thus in Hor. *Od.* 2. 16. 21:

> Scandit aeratas vitiosa puppes
> Cura...

What does *vitiosa* mean? Those who watch Horace at work
are aware how significant is his grouping together of epithets.
Here things that are *aeratas* are the objects of something that is
vitiosa. Then we remember that *vitium* may mean a flaw or

passim manus, 1. 21. 6 duo *deinceps* reges etc. (see my *Latin and English
Idiom*, p. 15). The sense must be "gravidam lateque patentem segetem."

In ll. 316-7 there are two good instances of Vergil's pointed order, i.e. *flavis*
and *fragili*. Both adjectives are prepositive and separated from their nouns.
The fields are yellow *flavis* (not green) for the reaper; they are "white to
the harvest"; the stalks are dry and brittle *fragili* (not soft and juicy) for
cutting.

As to l. 320, may not the original reading have been *eruerent, ut turbine
nigro*? The *ut* would easily drop out (...ENTVTTVRB...); then *ita* was introduced from a gloss on *ut* (i.e. *ut*=in such a way that) in order to make the
line scan.

crack, and we not unfairly assume that *vitiosa* means full of (and, by an easy transition, producing) such cracks and flaws, until we arrive at the interpretation "cankering"—an interpretation which, I think, is admirably suited to the context. Thus *vitiosa* is merely more picturesque than *edax*—Care eats even into the bronze of ships, into the "hearts of oak." But if I am right in my interpretation, Horace has interpreted for me by his happy juxtaposition of words.

And so in my commentary I shall continually draw attention to the order, because I am persuaded that, when Livy is writing at his best, every departure, however small, from normal order is of the highest importance, if we would understand the meaning aright.

I therefore conclude by giving the rules of *normal* order [1], viz. :

(*a*) Subject (1), object (2), verb (3), (sometimes we find these in the order (3), (2), (1)).

(*b*) Epithets of any kind (including the genitive case) immediately follow the word to which they belong, i.e. are "postpositive."

(*c*) Adjectives of number and quantity, demonstrative pronouns, and adverbs immediately precede the words to which they belong, i.e. are "prepositive."

(*d*) Coordinative and subordinative conjunctions, relative and interrogative pronouns or adverbs come first in their clause.

(*e*) A Latin sentence if *constructionally* complete must *ipso facto* be at an end.

---

[1] For details I refer the student to Professor Postgate's *Sermo Latinus*, pp. 35—45.

CHAPTER I

§ 1. Amid the anxieties caused by such serious wars either scarcely concluded or already threatening, there occurred an episode which, though trivial as narrative, occasioned so much feeling that it ended in a grave conflict. § 2. Marcus Fundanius and Lucius Valerius, plebeian tribunes, introduced before the Commons a proposal to repeal the Oppian law.

§ 3. This law had been passed on the motion of the tribune Gaius Oppius during the consulship of Quintus Fabius and Tiberius Sempronius, when the excitement of the Punic war was at its height. It provided that a woman should possess not more than half an ounce of gold, and wear no dresses of iridescent colours. Women were also forbidden to ride in carriages either in the city or in towns or within a mile's radius of these, except for purposes of state religious ceremonial.

§ 4. Marcus and Publius Junius Brutus, tribunes of the

§ 1. Inter bellorum magnorum aut vixdum finitorum aut imminentium curas intercessit res parva dictu, sed quae studiis in magnum certamen excesserit. § 2. M. Fundanius et L. Valerius tribuni plebi ad plebem tulerunt de Oppia lege abroganda.

§ 3. tulerat eam C. Oppius tribunus plebis Q. Fabio, Ti. Sempronio consulibus, in medio ardore Punici belli, ne qua mulier plus semunciam auri haberet nec vestimento versicolori uteretur neu iuncto vehiculo in urbe oppidove aut propius inde mille passus nisi sacrorum publicorum causa veheretur.

§ 4. M. et P. Iunii Bruti tribuni plebis legem Oppiam

plebs, championed the Oppian law, and asserted that they would not permit its repeal. In support or opposition came forward a large number of nobles, and the Capitol was filled with crowds of people upholding or condemning the measure.

§ 5. Deaf to the representations of their husbands, unmoved by respect for them or their bidding, married women could not be kept within doors. They besieged every road in the city and every approach to the forum, begging their husbands, as these descended thither, to remember the prosperity of the state, with the daily growth of all private fortunes, and to permit that their wives as well as themselves should have restored to them the adornments of the past. § 6. This concourse of the women increased day by day, as they gathered even from country towns and villages. § 7. And now they ventured to approach and solicit consuls, praetors, and other officials. But of the first, one at least, Marcus Porcius Cato, was found inexorable, and, in support of the law whose repeal was proposed, he delivered the following speech.

tuebantur nec eam se abrogari passuros aiebant ; ad suadendum dissuadendumque multi nobiles prodibant ; Capitolium turba hominum faventium adversantiumque legi complebatur.

§ 5. matronae nulla nec auctoritate nec verecundia nec imperio virorum contineri limine poterant, omnis vias urbis aditusque in forum obsidebant viros descendentis ad forum orantes, ut florente re publica, crescente in dies privata omnium fortuna, matronis quoque pristinum ornatum reddi paterentur. § 6. augebatur haec frequentia mulierum in dies ; nam etiam ex oppidis conciliabulisque conveniebant. § 7. iam et consules praetoresque et alios magistratus adire et rogare audebant ; ceterum minime exorabilem alterum utique consulem, M. Porcium Catonem, habebant, qui pro lege, quae abrogabatur, ita disseruit :

CHAPTER II

§ 1. "Gentlemen, if each of us in his relations with the mistress of his household had, from the beginning, retained the rights and prerogatives of a husband, we should now have less trouble with the other sex as a whole.

§ 2. Unfortunately in the home our liberties have been overthrown by undisciplined womanhood, and here also, in the forum, they are being trodden under foot. We have failed to curb individual women and therefore we tremble before them in the mass.

§ 3. For my own part, I always thought it a fabulous story that the whole male population in a certain island was once destroyed root and branch by a conspiracy among the women; § 4. but from every class and from both sexes we are in utmost danger, if cabals, meetings, and secret conclaves are permitted. Indeed *I* can scarcely decide in my own mind which is worse—the proposal itself, or the bad example set in carrying it into effect. § 5. Of the two, the latter concerns us, the consuls and other officials: the former rather concerns you, the burgesses of Rome. For whether the proposition before you conduces to the common weal

§ 1. "si in sua quisque nostrum matre familiae, Quirites, ius et maiestatem viri retinere instituisset, minus cum universis feminis negotii haberemus;

§ 2. nunc domi victa libertas nostra impotentia muliebri hic quoque in foro obteritur et calcatur, et, quia singulas non continuimus, universas horremus.

§ 3. equidem fabulam et fictam rem ducebam esse, virorum omne genus in aliqua insula coniuratione muliebri ab stirpe sublatum esse; § 4. ab nullo genere non summum periculum est, si coetus et concilia et secretas consultationes esse sinas. atque ego vix statuere apud animum meum possum, utrum peior ipsa res an peiore exemplo agatur; § 5. quorum alterum ad nos consules reliquosque magistratus, alterum ad vos, Quirites, magis pertinet. nam utrum e re publica sit necne id, quod ad vos fertur, vestra existimatio est, qui

or not, is a question for you to determine who are about to vote ; § 6. but this agitation by women, a spontaneous effort, it may be, or due to the influence of you, Marcus Fundanius, and you, Lucius Valerius (the blame for it, undoubtedly, rests on official shoulders)—this agitation is, I say, a disgrace ; whether a greater disgrace to you the tribunes, or to us the consuls, I do not know ; § 7. the shame is yours, if you have gone the length of bringing females here to excite tribunician disturbances : it is ours, if, like the plebs of old, the women are now to secede and dictate terms.

§ 8. Speaking for myself, it was not without a blush of shame that, a few moments ago, I made my way through a crowd of women into the forum. Had not respect for individual dignity and modesty (I had no respect for such females collectively) prevented me from letting them be seen scolded by a consul, I should have addressed them thus : § 9. 'What sort of practice is this—running out into the public streets, besieging the highways, and accosting the husbands of others ? Could not each of you have made this very request to your own lords and in the home ? § 10. Or are you more fascinating in public than in private, more fascinating to

in suffragium ituri estis ; § 6. haec consternatio muliebris, sive sua sponte, sive auctoribus vobis, M. Fundani et L. Valeri, facta est, haud dubie ad culpam magistratuum pertinens, nescio, vobis tribuni, an consulibus magis sit deformis : § 7. vobis, si feminas ad concitandas tribunicias seditiones iam adduxistis ; nobis, si ut plebis quondam, sic nunc mulierum secessione leges accipiendae sunt.

§ 8. equidem non sine rubore quodam paulo ante per medium agmen mulierum in forum perveni. quod nisi me verecundia singularum magis maiestatis et pudoris quam universarum tenuisset, ne compellatae a consule viderentur, dixissem : § 9. 'qui hic mos est in publicum procurrendi et obsidendi vias et viros alienos appellandi ? istud ipsum suos quaeque domi rogare non potuistis ? § 10. an blandiores in publico quam in

strangers than to your husbands? And yet, even in the home (if married women were restrained by modesty within the bounds of their due rights), it would have been seemly for you to care nothing what laws are passed or rejected in this place.'

§ 11. Our forefathers laid down that women should not transact any business, even of a private nature, without the authority of a guardian; they were to be under the control of parents, brother, or husband. But we, forsooth, allow them now actually to take part in politics, to appear in the forum, and to join in meetings and elections. § 12. For what are they doing, at this moment, in the streets and at the cross-roads, but supporting a proposal of the tribunes, and voting for the repeal of a law? § 13. Give free rein to a nature that knows no control, to a creature untamed, and hope that women, of themselves, will set a limit to extravagance of liberty. § 14. But unless *you* set such a limit, this is the least of the disabilities, imposed by custom or by law, under which women chafe. Liberty in all things, or rather, to speak plain truth, licence in all things, is what they desire.

privato et alienis quam vestris estis? quamquam ne domi quidem vos, si sui iuris finibus matronas contineret pudor, quae leges hic rogarentur abrogarenturve, curare decuit.'

§ 11. maiores nostri nullam, ne privatam quidem rem agere feminas sine tutore auctore voluerunt, in manu esse parentium, fratrum, virorum; nos, si diis placet, iam etiam rem publicam capessere eas patimur et foro quoque et contionibus et comitiis immisceri. § 12. quid enim nunc aliud per vias et compita faciunt, quam rogationem tribunorum plebi suadent, quam legem abrogandam censent? § 13. date frenos impotenti naturae et indomito animali et sperate ipsas modum licentiae facturas; § 14. nisi vos facietis, minimum hoc eorum est, quae iniquo animo feminae sibi aut moribus aut legibus iniuncta patiuntur. omnium rerum libertatem, immo licentiam, si vere dicere volumus, desiderant

CHAPTER III

§ 1. And if they carry this position, they will stop at nothing. Review women's rights and all the limitations by which your forefathers curbed their wilfulness and through which they subjected them to their husbands ; and yet, with all these restraints, you can scarcely keep them in check.

§ 2. Furthermore, if you suffer them to pluck and wrest from you privileges one by one, in the end allowing equality with men, think you that you will find them endurable ? No, the instant they begin to be your equals, they will get the upper hand.

§ 3. But, we are told, they take exception to a new measure directed against them : not law but outrage on law is the object of their protest. § 4. Nay rather, they demand that you should repeal a measure which by your votes you have accepted and enacted, a measure which the use and experience of so many years have stamped with your approval ; in fact, they ask you to abolish one law and so weaken all others. § 5. No enactment is acceptable to every citizen. The only question raised is : 'Does it benefit the majority ? Is it, in the main, of advantage ?' An individual may be privately offended by some

§ 1. quid enim, si hoc expugnaverint, non temptabunt ? recensete omnia muliebria iura, quibus licentiam earum adligaverint maiores vestri per quaeque subiecerint viris ; quibus omnibus constrictas vix tamen continere potestis.

§ 2. quid ? si carpere singula et extorquere et aequari ad extremum viris patiemini, tolerabiles vobis eas fore creditis ? extemplo, simul pares esse coeperint, superiores erunt.

§ 3. at hercule ne quid novum in eas rogetur recusant, non ius sed iniuriam deprecantur ; § 4. immo, ut, quam accepistis iussistis suffragiis vestris legem, quam usu tot annorum et experiendo comprobastis, hanc ut abrogetis, id est ut unam tollendo legem ceteras infirmetis. § 5. nulla lex satis commoda omnibus est ; id modo quaeritur, si maiori parti et in summam prodest. si, quod cuique privatim officiet ius, id destruet

legislation : is he therefore to pull it down in ruins? If so, what is the good of the community's passing laws which can so quickly be rescinded by those against whom they were directed?

§ 6. I should like, however, to hear why it is that married women have rushed hysterically into the public streets, all but invading forum and assembly. § 7. Is it to redeem from Hannibal prisoners of war, fathers, husbands, children, and brothers? Far is, and far for ever be, such a misfortune from our country! Yet, when such a misfortune did come, you refused this boon to their prayers of love and patriotism.

§ 8. But perhaps it is not love or anxiety for their dear ones that has gathered them here; it is religion : they are waiting to welcome the Holy Mother of Ida on Her way from Pessinus in Phrygia. No? Then what honourable plea, honourable at least in word, is put forward to excuse this revolt of our women? § 9. The reply comes : 'We wish to glitter in gold and purple, to ride in carriages every day, festival or no festival, to be carried through the city as if in triumph over a law vanquished and repealed, over your votes taken captive out of your hands. In fine, we ask that no limit should be set to extravagance and voluptuousness.'

ac demolietur, quid attinebit universos rogare leges, quas mox abrogare, in quos latae sunt, possint?

§ 6. volo tamen audire, quid sit, propter quod matronae consternatae procucurrerint in publicum ac vix foro se et contione abstineant. § 7. ut captivi ab Hannibale redimantur parentes, viri, liberi, fratres earum? procul abest absitque semper talis fortuna rei publicae; sed tamen, cum fuit, negastis hoc piis precibus earum.

§ 8. at non pietas nec sollicitudo pro suis, sed religio congregavit eas: matrem Idaeam a Pessinunte ex Phrygia venientem accepturae sunt. quid honestum dictu saltem seditioni praetenditur muliebri? § 9. 'ut auro et purpura fulgamus' inquit, 'ut carpentis festis profestisque diebus, velut triumphantes de lege victa et abrogata et captis et ereptis suffragiis vestris, per urbem vectemur; ne ullus modus sumptibus, ne luxuriae sit.'

CHAPTER IV

§ 1. You have often heard me complain about the expenses of women, and of men no less, and those not only private citizens but state officials also ; § 2. you have often heard me say that two opposite vices, greed and luxury, are endangering the state, curses which have proved the ruin of all great empires.   § 3. And this is what frightens me ; for the happier and more prosperous our country, and the greater the daily increase of our empire (already we have crossed into Greece and Asia Minor, both richly stored with every incentive to voluptuousness ; nay, our hands covet the treasures of eastern potentates)—the more do I dread the situation, and fear that our acquisitions have mastered us, not we them.   § 4. Believe me, these art treasures have come from Syracuse like an invading army against our city. Too many, even now, I hear full of praise and admiration for the ornaments of Corinth and of Athens, full of mockery for the clay figures of Rome's gods on the temple pediments.   § 5. But, for myself, I prefer these gods and their blessing, and I trust that they will grant it, if only we suffer them to remain in their old homes.

§ 1. saepe me querentem de feminarum, saepe de virorum nec de privatorum modo sed etiam magistratuum sumptibus audistis, § 2. diversisque duobus vitiis, avaritia et luxuria, civitatem laborare, quae pestes omnia magna imperia everterunt.   § 3. haec ego, quo melior laetiorque in dies fortuna rei publicae est imperiumque crescit—et iam in Graeciam Asiamque transcendimus omnibus libidinum illecebris repletas et regias etiam adtrectamus gazas—, eo plus horreo, ne illae magis res nos ceperint quam nos illas.   § 4. infesta, mihi credite, signa ab Syracusis illata sunt huic urbi. iam nimis multos audio Corinthi et Athenarum ornamenta laudantis mirantisque et antefixa fictilia deorum Romanorum ridentis. § 5. ego hos malo propitios deos et ita spero futuros, si in suis manere sedibus patiemur.

§ 6. Within the memory of our fathers, the envoy Cineas was employed by Pyrrhus in an attempt to bribe not only men, but women also. The Oppian law had not yet been passed to curb feminine luxuriousness; for all that, not one woman accepted a bribe. § 7. And what, think you, was the reason? The same reason which led our ancestors to make no legal provision in the matter: there existed no luxuriousness to be curbed. § 8. Just as we must diagnose the disease before we can know the remedy, so evil desires come into existence before the laws which are to limit them. § 9. What called forth the Licinian law, with its restriction of 500 acres, except inordinate passion for enlarging estates? What the Cincian law against gifts and presents, except that the plebs had now commenced to be the pensioners and dependents of the senate? § 10. Thus there is little reason to wonder that neither the Oppian law nor any other was wanted to limit the extravagances of women, when they refused to accept gold and purple, freely given, nay thrust upon them. § 11. But, to-day, had Cineas gone the round of the city with his bribes, he would have found women standing in the public streets to receive them.

§ 6. patrum nostrorum memoria per legatum Cineam Pyrrhus non virorum modo sed etiam mulierum animos donis temptavit. nondum lex Oppia ad coercendam luxuriam muliebrem lata erat; tamen nulla accepit. § 7. quam causam fuisse censetis? eadem fuit, quae maioribus nostris nihil de hac re lege sanciundi; nulla erat luxuria, quae coerceretur. § 8. sicut ante morbos necesse est cognitos esse quam remedia earum, sic cupiditates prius natae sunt quam leges, quae iis modum facerent. § 9. quid legem Liciniam excitavit de quingentis iugeribus nisi ingens cupido agros continuandi? quid legem Cinciam de donis et muneribus, nisi quia vectigalis iam et stipendiaria plebs esse senatui coeperat? § 10. itaque minime mirum est nec Oppiam nec aliam ullam tum legem desideratam esse, quae modum sumptibus mulierum faceret, cum aurum et purpuram data et oblata ultro non accipiebant. § 11. si nunc cum illis donis Cineas urbem circumiret, stantis in publico invenisset, quae acciperent.

§ 12.   Indeed for some desires
I cannot find even the ground or
the motive. Granting that the
denial of what is lawful for one's
neighbour brings with it some
perhaps not unnatural feeling of
shame or vexation, still, when
fashions are the same for all,
wherein need each one of you
ladies fear to be made conspicuous?
§ 13.   The lowest shame is shame
of thrift or humble circumstances;
but the law takes from you both
forms of shame, when you do not
possess that which it is unlawful
to have.

§ 14.   'But,' says our wealthy
lady, 'it is just this equality that
I cannot endure. Why may I not
attract attention by a blaze of
purple and gold? Why should the
poor circumstances of other women
find concealment under this pretext of a law, making it seem that
what they cannot afford they might
have had but for legislation?'
§ 15.   Gentlemen, do you wish
such rivalry to be instilled in your
wives as will cause the rich to
desire only what no one else of
their sex can have, and the poor,
fearing contempt on this very
ground, to overstrain their means?
§ 16.   Assuredly, so soon as *they*
feel shame where shame should
not exist, they will cease to feel it
where it should. The woman who
possesses the means will get her

§ 12.   atque ego nonnullarum
cupiditatium ne causam quidem
aut rationem inire possum.   nam
ut, quod alii liceat, tibi non licere
aliquid fortasse naturalis aut pudoris aut indignationis habeat, sic
aequato omnium cultu quid una-
quaeque vestrum veretur ne in
se conspiciatur?   § 13. pessimus
quidem pudor est vel parsimoniae
vel paupertatis; sed utrumque lex
vobis demit, cum id quod habere
non licet, non habetis.

§ 14.   'hanc' inquit 'ipsam
exaequationem non fero' illa locuples.   'cur non insignis auro et
purpura conspicior? cur paupertas
aliarum sub hac legis specie latet,
ut, quod habere non possunt, habi-
turae, si liceret, fuisse videantur?'
§ 15.   vultis hoc certamen uxoribus vestris inicere, Quirites, ut
divites id habere velint, quod nulla
alia possit; pauperes, ne ob hoc
ipsum contemnantur, supra vires
se extendant?   § 16. ne *eas* simul
pudere, quod non oportet, coeperit,
quod oportet, non pudebit.   quae

desire, the woman who does not will ask her husband. § 17. Unhappy man, whether he yield to her prayers or not! What he does not give himself, he will see given by another. § 18. Even now they frequently solicit the husbands of others, and, what is more, they ask for a measure and for votes, and get them, too, in certain quarters. But it is to the detriment of yourself, Sir, your property, and your children, that you are compliant; once let the law cease to limit the expenses of your wife, and *you* will never succeed in doing it.

§ 19. Do not imagine, gentlemen, that the position will be the same as it was before the law was passed to deal with it. It is less dangerous for a bad man to escape trial than to be acquitted; and luxury unawaked would have been more tolerable than it will be now, —maddened, like some wild beast, by its very chains, and then let loose.

§ 20. I therefore move that the Oppian law by no means be repealed; but whatever course you adopt, may the blessing of every god rest upon it!"

de suo poterit, parabit, quae non poterit, virum rogabit. § 17. miserum illum virum, et qui exoratus et qui non exoratus erit, cum, quod ipse non dederit, datum ab alio videbit. § 18. nunc vulgo alienos viros rogant et, quod maius est, legem et suffragia rogant et a quibusdam impetrant. adversus te et rem tuam et liberos tuos exorabilis es; simul lex modum sumptibus uxoris tuae facere desierit, tu numquam facies.

§ 19. nolite eodem loco existimare, Quirites, futuram rem, quo fuit, antequam lex de hoc ferretur. et hominem improbum non accusari tutius est quam absolvi, et luxuria non mota tolerabilior esset, quam erit nunc, ipsis vinculis, sicut ferae bestiae, irritata, deinde emissa.

§ 20. ego nullo modo abrogandam legem Oppiam censeo; vos quod faxitis, deos omnis fortunare velim."

CHAPTER V

§ 1. After this speech those plebeian tribunes who had promised their intervention added a few words to the same purport. Then Lucius Valerius addressed the assembly in support of the bill which he himself had brought forward.

"If," he said, "private members only had risen to speak for or against the measure before us, I, for my part, feeling that enough had been said on both sides, should have remained silent and awaited the verdict of your votes. § 2. But since a gentleman of such authority, and a consul—I mean Marcus Porcius—has not only used the weight of his influence, which needed no words to enhance it, but has also delivered a lengthy and carefully prepared oration against our proposal, I am compelled to make a brief reply. § 3. The consul, however, expended more verbiage on reproof of married women than on criticism of our bill ; and he actually raised the question whether the course which he blamed had been adopted by these ladies of their own accord or at our instigation. § 4. But it is the measure that I propose to defend, not ourselves, against whom the consul levelled this

§ 1. Post haec tribuni quoque plebi, qui se intercessuros professi erant cum pauca in eandem sententiam adiecissent, tum L. Valerius pro rogatione ab se promulgata ita disseruit :

"si privati tantummodo ad suadendum dissuadendumque id, quod ab nobis rogatur, processissent, ego quoque, cum satis dictum pro utraque parte existimarem, tacitus suffragia vestra exspectassem ; § 2. nunc cum vir gravissimus, consul M. Porcius, non auctoritate solum, quae tacita satis momenti habuisset, sed oratione etiam longa et accurata insectatus sit rogationem nostram, necesse est paucis respondere. § 3. qui tamen plura verba in castigandis matronis quam in rogatione nostra dissuadenda consumpsit, et quidem ut in dubio poneret, utrum id, quod reprehenderet, matronae sua sponte an nobis auctoribus fecissent. § 4. rem defendam, non nos, in quos

allegation, though without any evidence to support his charge. § 5. He talked of conspiracy, sedition, and sometimes secession on the part of the women, because our wives publicly asked that a law whose passage was aimed against them in time of war and during a period of distress should be repealed by you, now that peace reigns and the state is prosperous and flourishing.

§ 6. These and other flights of rhetoric I know there are, to be pressed into the service of exaggeration ; and we are all aware that M. Cato, as a speaker, is not merely weighty, but, sometimes, aggressive too, despite his gentle character. § 7. For what startling novelty have these ladies introduced by crowding the streets and courting publicity in a matter which touches them so nearly ? Is this the first time upon which they have appeared before the public gaze ? Nay, I will open your own ' Antiquities' and refute you from it. § 8. Hear how often they have done the same thing, and always to the interests of the state. To begin at the beginning— in the reign of Romulus, when the Sabines had seized the Capitol and a pitched battle was being fought in the very midst of the forum, did not the matrons rush between the two lines and stay the fury of the fight ?

iecit magis hoc consul verbo tenus, quam ut re insimularet. § 5. coetum et seditionem et interdum secessionem muliebrem appellavit, quod matronae in publico vos rogassent, ut legem in se latam per bellum temporibus duris in pace et florenti ac beata re publica abrogaretis.

§ 6. uerba magna, quae rei augendae causa conquirantur, haec et alia esse scio, et M. Catonem oratorem non solum gravem sed interdum etiam trucem esse scimus omnes, cum ingenio sit mitis. § 7. nam quid tandem novi matronae fecerunt, quod frequentes in causa ad se pertinente in publicum processerunt ? numquam ante hoc tempus in publico apparuerunt ? tuas adversus te Origines revolvam. § 8. accipe quotiens id fecerint, et quidem semper bono publico, iam a principio, regnante Romulo, cum Capitolio ab Sabinis capto medio in foro signis collatis dimicaretur, nonne intercursu matronarum inter acies duas proelium sedatum est ?

§ 9. Again, after the expulsion of the kings, when Marcius Coriolanus, at the head of the Volscian legions, had encamped within five miles, was it not *they* who turned away the army, which, otherwise, would have overwhelmed this city? Furthermore, when it had been taken by the Gauls, was not its ransom the gold which *they* contributed to the treasury amid universal applause? § 10. And, not to go to ancient history, in the last war, when there was need of money, did not the widows and the unmarried assist the public funds from their own? And also, when new deities were called in to aid our desperate fortunes, did not our matrons, one and all, set forth to the sea that they might greet the Holy Mother of Ida?

§ 11. But, say you, the grounds are different. Well, I have not set out to prove them parallel. It is sufficient to make good my plea that nothing unprecedented has been done. § 12. If, however, under conditions which affected everybody—men and women alike —no one marvelled at what the matrons did, why, in a case which especially touches themselves, should we wonder at their action? § 13. But what has that action been? Upon my soul, our ears are the ears of tyrants, if, when masters do not disdain the prayers

§ 9. quid? regibus exactis cum Coriolano Marcio duce legiones Volscorum castra ad quintum lapidem posuissent, nonne id agmen, quo obruta haec urbs esset, matronae averterunt? iam urbe capta a Gallis aurum, quo redempta urbs est, nonne matronae consensu omnium in publicum contulerunt? § 10. proximo bello, ne antiqua repetam, nonne et, cum pecunia opus fuit, viduarum pecuniae adiuverunt aerarium, et, cum dii quoque novi ad opem ferendam dubiis rebus accerserentur, matronae universae ad mare profectae sunt ad matrem Idaeam accipiendam?

§ 11. dissimiles, inquis, causae sunt. nec mihi causas aequare propositum est; nihil novi factum purgare satis est. § 12. ceterum quod in rebus ad omnis pariter, viros feminas, pertinentibus fecisse eas nemo miratus est, in causa proprie ad ipsas pertinente miramur fecisse? § 13. quid autem fecerunt? superbas, me dius fidius, aures habemus, si, cum domini servorum non fastidiant

of their slaves, we are scandalised by the entreaties of honourable women.

preces, nos rogari ab honestis feminis indignamur.

CHAPTER VI

§ 1. And now I come to the question at issue. Here the consul's speech fell under two heads : first he strongly objected to the repeal of any law whatsoever; secondly to the repeal, in particular, of a law for the repression of female extravagances.

§ 2. This universal defence of legislation seemed a fit topic for a consul; while the attack on luxury was well-suited to an austere morality.   § 3. Thus there is danger that dust may be thrown in your eyes, unless we show the fallacy which underlies each objection.   § 4. Speaking for myself, I admit that laws which are passed, not to meet some special need, but to stand for all time because of their permanent utility, should in no case be repealed, unless either experience has proved them a mistake, or some particular condition of the body politic has rendered them nugatory. § 5. On the other hand, laws once demanded by special situations I see to be "mortal" (if I may use the word) and liable to change with

§ 1. Venio nunc ad id, de quo agitur. in quo duplex consulis oratio fuit ; nam et legem ullam omnino abrogari est indignatus, et eam praecipue legem, quae luxuriae muliebris coercendae causa lata esset.

§ 2. et illa communis pro legibus visa consularis oratio est, et haec adversus luxuriam severissimis moribus conveniebat. § 3. itaque periculum est, nisi, quid in utraque re vani sit, docuerimus, ne quis error vobis offundatur.   § 4. ego enim quem ad modum ex iis legibus, quae non in tempus aliquid, sed perpetuae utilitatis causa in aeternum latae sunt, nullam abrogari debere fateor, nisi quam aut usus coarguit aut status aliquis rei publicae inutilem fecit,   § 5. sic, quas tempora aliqua desiderarunt leges, mortales, ut ita dicam, et temporibus ipsis mutabiles esse video.

2—2

changing times. § 6. Measures
adopted in peace are generally
rescinded by war; those adopted
in war, by peace. In directing a
ship, some methods are of value
for good weather, others for bad.
§ 7. Since then these two types
of legislation are inherently so
different, to which type, think
you, does this law whose repeal
we propose belong? § 8. Well,
is it some ancient enactment of
the kings, as old as the life of our
city? Or, to take the era following,
when the decemvirs were appointed
to draw up a code, was it included
by them in the Twelve Tables?
Did our ancestors regard it as
essential to the preservation of
wifely honour, and therefore must
we fear that, in annulling it, we
annul also the purity and sanctity
of womanhood?

§ 9. But everyone knows that
this is a law without precedent,
carried twenty years ago in the
consulship of Quintus Fabius and
Tiberius Sempronius. Without it,
for all those years, married women
lived lives beyond reproach; and
why, pray, is there danger that its
repeal may lead to an outbreak of
voluptuousness? § 10. If this
measure had been one of long
standing, or passed in order to
limit feminine indulgence, there
would be reason to fear that its
abolition might prove an incite-

§ 6. quae in pace lata sunt, plerumque bellum abrogat, quae in
bello pax, ut in navis administratione alia in secunda, alia in
adversa tempestate usui sunt.
§ 7. haec cum ita natura distincta sint, ex utro tandem genere
ea lex esse videtur, quam abrogamus? § 8. quid? vetus regia
lex, simul cum ipsa urbe nata aut,
quod secundum est, ab decemviris
ad condenda iura creatis in duodecim tabulis scripta, sine qua
cum maiores nostri non existimarint decus matronale servari
posse, nobis quoque verendum sit,
ne cum ea pudorem sanctitatemque feminarum abrogemus?

§ 9. quis igitur nescit novam
istam legem esse, Q. Fabio et Ti.
Sempronio consulibus viginti ante
annis latam? sine qua cum per
tot annos matronae optimis moribus vixerint, quod tandem, ne
abrogata ea effundantur ad luxuriam, periculum est? § 10. nam
si ista lex *vetus* aut ideo lata esset,
ut finiret libidinem muliebrem,
verendum foret, ne abrogata in-

ment; but the grounds of its adoption may be seen in the circumstances themselves. § 11. Hannibal was in Italy, the victor of Cannae; Tarentum, Arpi, and Capua were already in his hands; § 12. Rome itself was thought to be the objective of his army; our allies had revolted; there were no soldiers to take the place of the fallen, no seamen to man the fleet, no money in the treasury; slaves were being purchased to bear arms, the price for whom was to be paid to their owners on the conclusion of hostilities; § 13. up to the same date of settlement the tax-farmers promised to contract for the supply of corn and other necessaries of war; slaves to act as rowers, the number fixed in proportion to income, were being provided by us as well as pay; § 14. all our gold and silver (senators had set the example) we were contributing to the public service; widows, unmarried women, and wards were taking what they possessed to the treasury; it was provided by law that we should have at home not more than a certain amount of wrought gold and silver, or of silver and bronze coin—: § 15. at such a time, were the wives so given up to luxurious adornment that the Oppian law was needed for its repression? Why, owing to the

citaret; cur sit autem lata, ipsum indicabit tempus. § 11. Hannibal in Italia erat, victor ad Cannas; iam Tarentum, iam Arpos, iam Capuam habebat; § 12. ad urbem Romam admoturus exercitum videbatur; defecerant socii; non milites in supplementum, non socios navalis ad classem tuendam, non pecuniam in aerario habebamus; servi, quibus arma darentur, ita ut pretium pro iis bello perfecto dominis solveretur, emebantur; § 13. in eandem diem pecuniae frumentum et cetera, quae belli usus postulabant, praebenda publicani se conducturos professi erant; servos ad remum numero ex censu constituto cum stipendio nostro dabamus; § 14. aurum et argentum omne ab senatoribus eius rei initio orto in publicum conferebamus; viduae et pupilli pecunias suas in aerarium deferebant; cautum erat, quo ne plus auri et argenti facti, quo ne plus signati argenti et aeris domi haberemus—: § 15. tali tempore in luxuria et ornatu matronae occupatae erant, ut ad eam coercendam Oppia lex desiderata sit,

abandonment of Ceres' sacrifice (for all the women were in mourning), the senate commanded that the period of such mourning should be limited to thirty days !

§ 16. Anyone can see that the poverty and distress in the country, when every private citizen had to convert his money to the public use, were responsible for this piece of legislation which was to remain on the statute book only so long as the reason for its enactment continued to exist.

§ 17. For if the measures then decreed by the senate or passed by the assembly to meet the circumstances of the moment ought to hold good for all time, why do we refund moneys to private persons ? Why do we call for state contracts on the basis of immediate payment ? § 18. Why are slaves not bought to serve in our armies ? Why do we not, as individuals, provide rowers, exactly as we provided them before ?

cum, quia Cereris sacrificium lugentibus omnibus matronis intermissum erat, senatus finiri luctum triginta diebus iussit?

§ 16. cui non apparet inopiam et miseriam civitatis, [et] quia omnium privatorum pecuniae in usum publicum vertendae erant, istam legem scripsisse, tam diu mansuram, quam diu causa scribendae legis mansisset ?

§ 17. nam si, quae tunc temporis causa aut decrevit senatus aut populus iussit, in perpetuum servari oportet, cur pecunias reddimus privatis ? cur publica praesenti pecunia locamus? § 18. cur servi, qui militent, non emuntur ? cur privati non damus remiges, sicut tunc dedimus ?

CHAPTER VII

§ 1. All other classes, all other persons are to feel the improvement in the condition of the state ; and shall only our wives reap no benefit from its peace and tranquillity ? § 2. Purple will be worn

§ 1. omnes alii ordines, omnes homines mutationem in meliorem statum rei publicae sentient ; ad coniuges tantum nostras pacis et tranquillitatis publicae fructus non perveniet ? § 2. purpura viri

by us men in the official dress of magistrates and priests; our children will wear the toga bordered with purple; magistrates in colonies and provincial towns, and here, in Rome, the lowest official class, the superintendents of streets, will receive from us the right to use this same dress; § 3. and not merely in life may they have this uniform : when dead they may be cremated with it. Shall we then deny the use of purple to none but women ? You, the husband, may have purple for your hangings, and will you not allow the mistress of your household to wear that colour in her mantle ? Are the caparisons of your horse to be more brilliant than the dresses of your wife ?

§ 4. Yet, in the case of purple, which wears out and is wasted, I can see that there is some reason, however unjust, for parsimony. But in the matter of gold, where, if we except the cost of workmanship, there is no loss in value, why should we be grudging ? Rather it is a safe investment for private and public needs, as, in fact, you have found out by experience.

§ 5. It was urged that no rivalry exists between individual women now that none of them possesses gold. But, surely, our women as a class feel the bitterest indignation when they see the

utemur, praetextati in magistratibus, in sacerdotiis ; liberi nostri praetextis purpura togis utentur ; magistratibus in coloniis municipiisque, hic Romae infimo generi, magistris vicorum, togae praetextae habendae ius permittemus, § 3. nec ut vivi solum habeant [tantum] insigne, sed etiam ut cum eo crementur mortui : feminis dumtaxat purpurae usu interdicemus ? et, cum tibi viro liceat purpura in vestem stragulam uti, matrem familiae tuam purpureum amiculum habere non sines, et equus tuus speciosius instratus erit quam uxor vestita ?

§ 4. sed in purpura, quae teritur absumitur, iniustam quidem, sed aliquam tamen causam tenacitatis video ; in auro vero, in quo praeter manupretium nihil intertrimenti fit, quae malignitas est ? praesidium potius in eo est et ad privatos et ad publicos usus, sicut experti estis.

§ 5. nullam aemulationem inter se singularum, quoniam nulla haberet, esse aiebat. at hercule universis dolor et indignatio est,

wives of Latin allies permitted such ornaments as are denied to themselves ; § 6. when they see them conspicuous in gold and purple, and driving through the city, while they themselves follow on foot, as if the administration were centred not in their own community but in the communities from which those others come. § 7. Such a contrast could wound the feelings of men ; how much more of weak women, who are affected by the merest trifles ?

§ 8. Offices, priesthoods, triumphs, decorations, donatives and spoils of war cannot fall to their lot ; § 9. toilet, ornaments, dress —these are the "decorations" of womanhood ; these are their delight and pride ; these are what our forefathers called "the adornment of woman."

§ 10. In mourning, what do they do but lay aside their gold as well as their purple ? When mourning is over, what do they do but resume them ? If they give thanks or offer supplications, what do they add save greater splendour in apparel ?

§ 11. Of course, if you repeal the Oppian law, *you* will be powerless should you desire to enforce any prohibition now contained in that law ! Of course, our daughters, wives, and even sisters will be less under control in certain

cum sociorum Latini nominis uxoribus vident ea concessa ornamenta, quae sibi adempta sint, § 6. cum insignis eas esse auro et purpura, cum illas vehi per urbem, se pedibus sequi, tamquam in illarum civitatibus, non in sua imperium sit. § 7. virorum hoc animos vulnerare posset ; quid muliercularum censetis, quas etiam parva movent ?

§ 8. non magistratus nec sacerdotia nec triumphi nec insignia nec dona aut spolia bellica iis contingere possunt ; § 9. munditiae et ornatus et cultus, haec feminarum insignia sunt, his gaudent et gloriantur, hunc mundum muliebrem appellarunt maiores nostri.

§ 10. quid aliud in luctu quam purpuram atque aurum deponunt ? quid, cum eluxerunt, sumunt ? quid in gratulationibus supplicationibusque nisi excellentiorem ornatum adiciunt ?

§ 11. scilicet, si legem Oppiam abrogaritis, non vestri arbitrii erit, si quid eius vetare volueritis, quod nunc lex vetat ; minus filiae, uxores, sorores etiam quibusdam

households ! § 12. But never, while their male relatives are living, is the yoke of slavery taken from women ; and they themselves abhor the liberty which is brought by the loss of husband or father. § 13. They desire that you, rather than the law, should regulate their adornment ; and you, on your part, should have them under protection and guardianship, not hold them in bondage, preferring the title of father or husband to that of master.

§ 14. Those were inflammatory expressions for a consul to use when just now he talked of sedition and secession on the part of the women. The danger is that they may seize the Sacred Hill— an angry plebs once did it—or perhaps the Aventine !

§ 15. But submission is for weakness like theirs, no matter what you decide. Yet the greater your power, the more moderate should be your exercise of it."

in manu erunt ;—§ 12. numquam salvis suis exuitur servitus muliebris ; et ipsae libertatem, quam viduitas et orbitas facit, detestantur. § 13. in vestro arbitrio suum ornatum quam in legis malunt esse ; et vos in manu et tutela, non in servitio debetis habere eas et malle patres vos aut viros quam dominos dici.

§ 14. invidiosis nominibus utebatur modo consul seditionem muliebrem et secessionem appellando. id enim periculum est, ne Sacrum montem, sicut quondam irata plebs, aut Aventinum capiant ;—

§ 15. patiendum huic infirmitati est, quodcumque vos censueritis. quo plus potestis, eo moderatius imperio uti debetis."

CHAPTER VIII

§ 1. Such were the speeches made in favour of or against the law.

Crowds of women, in larger numbers than ever, poured, next day, into the streets. § 2. A mass

§ 1. Haec cum contra legem proque lege dicta essent, aliquanto maior frequentia mulierum postero die sese in publicum effudit, § 2. unoque agmine omnes Bru-

meeting besieged the doors of the Bruti, who were attempting to block their colleagues' proposal. The women persisted in these methods until opposition was abandoned by the tribunes. § 3. There was then no doubt that the Lex Oppia would be repealed by all the tribes ; and repealed it was twenty years after it first became law.

torum ianuas obsederunt, qui collegarum rogationi intercedebant, nec ante abstiterunt, quam remissa intercessio ab tribunis est. § 3. nulla deinde dubitatio fuit, quin omnes tribus legem abrogarent. viginti annis post abrogata est quam lata.

CHAPTER I

§ 1. anxieties caused by... wars

= bellorum...curas—the genitive is a subjective genitive, like *hostium* in *terror hostium* = "the panic caused by the enemy."

such serious

= *magnorum* : the adjective of quantity is, abnormally, post-positive, and therefore has stress. Livy wishes to draw our attention to a double antithesis, viz., serious wars and trivial (*parva* post-positive) discussions.

The order *inter bellorum...curas* is to be observed. A Roman would read this : "Amid such wars... and their anxieties."

For the method of expression, compare 27. 8. 1 inter maiorum rerum curas comitia maximi curionis...vetus excitaverunt certamen. W. quotes 9. 30. 10 haec inter duorum ingentium bellorum curam gerebantur.

there occurred

= *intercessit*.

The verb in this sense of " intervened " is found with *inter* only here in Livy (W.).

an episode

= *res*.

For other meanings of this " blank cheque " see Index.

which though trivial as narrative ...ended in a grave conflict

= parva dictu, sed quae...in magnum certamen excesserit.

For the form of expression, i.e. an adjective combined with a relative + a consecutive subjunctive (the relative being equivalent to *talis ut*), cp. 6. 35. 5. "All measures of importance and measures which could not be carried without a very serious conflict " = cuncta ingentia et quae sine certamine maximo obtineri non possent.

W. quotes many parallels at 10. 23. 9.

trivial { as narrative
{ historically

= *parva dictu*

Lit. "small in point of the saying." Almost every verb has a verbal noun of the 4th Declension type, possessing only two cases, the accusative and ablative. The former is restricted to an accusative of "motion to" without a preposition, as in the survival *Romam* = to Rome (hence the so-called supine in *-um* occurs only with an idea of motion, cp. 34. 13. 2 praedatum milites in hostium agros ducebat); the latter is exclusively used as an ablative "in point of which," cp. 34. 3. 8 honestum dictu.

The terms "active" and "passive" supine should be abandoned. Even "supine" is almost meaningless ; but, until there is evidence to the contrary, I shall believe that *supinum* is a poor representative of κλιτικόν and simply signifies "declinable" (part of the verb).

which...occasioned so much feeling that it ended

=quae studiis...excesserit

Lit. "which by reason of party feeling ended...."

The plural *studia*=instances of *studium*, i.e. of partizanship. So *irae*=displays, outbreaks of anger. Compare Cic. *De Off.* 1. 22. 78 domesticae fortitudines= instances of civic courage ; *ib.* 1. 29. 103 quietibus ceteris=other modes of resting ; *ib.* 1. 36. 131 in festinationibus=in cases of hurry ; *ib.* 3. 16. 67 huiusmodi reticentiae =such cases of reticence. Add *De Amic.* § 69 excellentiae and *ib.* § 67 satietates. Dr Postgate (*Sermo Latinus*, § 61, p. 52) quotes a beautiful instance from Cic. *N. D.* ii, § 98.

Often the presence of a plural concrete genitive seems to produce plurality in the abstract noun. Thus "Guilty consciousness of such offences" becomes *conscientias eiusmodi facinorum* (Cic. *Pro Cluent.* 20. 56). Compare *Verr.* 5. 9. 23 *formidines...incommodorum* ; *Parad.* 2. 18 *conscientiae...maleficiorum.* Add *Rosc. Amer.* 24. 67.

ended in

=in (aliquid) excedere, cp. Greek τελευτᾶν ἔς τι.

grave

=magnum, despite *magnorum* above.

Latin has no objection to re-

petition. For other instances see
Index s. v. Repetition.

§ 2.

Note the repetition *plebi ad
plebem*)(English.

For *plebi*, an old form of the
genitive, surviving in this phrase
and in *plebiscitum*, see R. 1.
357 (*d*).

introduced a proposal

=tulerunt.

The full phrase would be *rogationem ferre* (*promulgare*); but in
the case of *ferre*, the noun is often
omitted.

to repeal the Oppian law

=de Oppia lege abroganda.

The rule of a Latin sentence is
that when *constructionally* complete it ought *ipso facto* to be at
an end.   Anything which then
lapses over gains great emphasis.
But here the sentence is not constructionally complete at *tulerunt*:
we still wait for *de*.   Hence there
is nothing abnormal in the order,
save that *Oppia* precedes *lege*.
Perhaps Livy wishes to avoid the
assonance Oppi*a* abrogand*a*.

The Oppian law had been
passed in 215 B.C.—twenty years
before the present proposal to
repeal it.

§ 3. This law had been passed
on the motion of Gaius Oppius

=tulerat eam C. Oppius.

Here *tulerat* acts as a connective by re-echoing *tulerunt*, as
in the familiar: "He took and
burnt the city"=urbem cepit:
captam incendit.

Distinguish *rogationem ferre*=
"propose a measure," and *legem*

ferre (*perferre*) = "get a law passed."

This C. (before Oppius) is the old letter which once stood both for C and G. It survived *when standing alone* in praenomina and represented G. Hence C. = Gaius. There is no such name as Caius.

Note the order—verb (*tulerat*), object (*eam*), subject (*Oppius*). This order is by no means uncommon, especially with *movere*, cp. 2. 13. 2 ; 2. 27. 3, etc. I have noticed at least 21 instances with *movere*.

during the consulship of Q. Fabius and Ti. Sempronius

= consulibus Q. Fabio, Ti. Sempronio.

Note that the abstract "consulship" becomes concrete "consuls" (cp. 34. 2. 6 *auctoribus*), and that Latin often omits "and" in such a phrase. For the "bimembral asyndeton" see M. § 434. But at 34. 6. 9 we have Q. Fabio et Ti. Sempronio consulibus.

when the excitement of the Punic War was at its height

= in medio ardore Punici belli.

Observe the prep. *in* expressing attendant circumstances, cp. *in re trepida*, and 34. 46. 12 "Where the struggle is desperate" = *in asperis rebus*.

The normal position of *Punici belli* would be between *medio* and *ardore*. Livy repeats the order of our text at 24. 45. 4 *in medio ardore belli* (but Curtius, 8. 4. 27 *in medio cupiditatis ardore*). Indeed when Livy has written preposition + adjective (or equivalent) + noun, the complement often lapses over, cp. 34. 2. 8 *per medium agmen mulierum* ; 36. 18. 3 *sub ipsis radicibus montis* ; 38. 22. 3 *in talibus iniquitatibus locorum* ; 31. 18. 7 *per omnes vias leti* ; 34. 14. 7 *ab dextro latere hostium* ; 34. 6. 13 *in eandem diem pecuniae.* Add 3. 10. 7 ; 7. 10. 8 ; 21. 21. 8 ; 23. 21. 2 ; 24. 45. 4 ; 38. 21. 1 ; 45. 6. 4 ; 45. 10. 10 etc. Similarly when one complement has already been inserted the other is allowed to lapse over, as always in Greek, e.g. αἱ ἐν τῷ λιμένι νῆες ὁρμοῦσαι, cp. 3. 40. 3 *foederis nefarie icti cum collegis,* and 21. 52. 6 *ob nimiam cultorum fidem in Romanos.*

Distinguish cases like 34. 9. 5 *partem muri versam in agros,* and 36. 10. 7 *urbis sitae in plano.* Here the sense is not complete at *versam* and *sitae,* and the words following do not come as a surprise.

See too note on 34. 1. 5 *omnes vias urbis.*

excitement of the war = ardor belli.

Metaphors from fires—which were of frequent occurrence in ancient cities—are very common in Latin ; so common that they were becoming dead metaphors. Thus at 21. 58. 6 a downpour of *rain* is said to set on fire (!) the violence of the wind—*effuso imbre*

...*eo magis accensa vis venti est.*
We say: "a heavy downpour
only *increased* the violence of the
wind."

Modern cities are built to
minimise the possibility of fires,
and the metaphor is consequently
strange to us. Thus we are content to say : "a serious war *broke
out*," where Livy (35. 2. 3) writes :
bellum ingens exarsit (cp. 40. 58. 2 ;
41. 25. 8).

In the same way, "a fierce
battle *began*"=*atrox pugna...ac-
censa est* (27. 32. 5, and compare
6. 3. 8 ; 9. 39. 6) ; "a furious
conflict *arose*"=*atrox proelium...
exarsit* (27. 2. 8) ; "the plague *de-
vastated* both city and country"=
*pestilentia urens simul urbem atque
agros* (10. 47. 6).

It provided that a woman should
possess not more

=*ne qua mulier plus...haberet.*

No new verb is needed in Latin.
The terms of the bill can depend
on *tulerat*, and the negative of
English comes to the very front in
Latin. We say: "*And*, on the
morrow, he spoke *not* a word";
Latin says : *nec quicquam postridie
dixit.*

Here *ne...haberet* explains *legem*
preceding, i.e. "a law that no
woman was to wear." We might
have had *ut ne*, where *ut* is ex-
planatory="namely that," and *ne
...haberet* is dependent jussive, representing *ne qua...habeat* of the
proclamation.

more than half an ounce

= plus semunciam.

The construction is as with *plus quam*. This is especially common with *plus* and *amplius* where numerals follow. See M. § 305.

and wear *no* dresses

= nec vestimento...uteretur.

For *nec* cp. above on *ne qua mulier*.

The combination *nĕ...nec* for *ne...neve* is not infrequent at all periods. Livy has one case of *ne ...ve* for *ne...neve*, viz. 43. 16. 2. Here he revels in a variety (*ne... nec...neu...aut*) which would have shocked Cicero.

Women were also forbidden to ride

= *neu*...veheretur.

"Women were also forbidden to" is mere English variety for "and (it provided that)...not (any woman) should." Latin continues the original construction without any sense of monotony. Similarly, in long passages of Or. Obl., English must continually insert such expressions as : "He also asserted," "he further urged," "he concluded by saying," etc.

in carriages

= iuncto vehiculo.

The preposition *in* is never required if the idea of the means (as here), the instrument, or the manner is involved. The full phrase is *vehiculo equis* (or *iumentis*) *iuncto* i.e. a vehicle yoked to horses (or beasts of burden). It is impossible to say whether *equis* is dative or ablative. Livy has the abbreviated expression *iuncta vehicula* at 42. 65. 3 also.

either in the city or in towns

=in urbe oppidove.

Here *urbe*=Rome, and *oppido* =any Roman provincial town.

Latin keeps the singular *oppido* to preserve parallelism.

Note *ve* the least emphatic word for " or." Its function is often, as here, to express a minor alternative within a major. Compare 21. 35. 2 utcumque *aut* locus opportunitatem daret *aut* progressi morati*ve* aliquam occasionem fecissent ; 1. 13. 7 id non traditur...*an* dignitatibus suis virorum*ve an* sorte lectae sint. See *C. R.* Vol. XVII. p. 43.

Similarly *vel...vel* may subdivide an *aut*, cp. Cic. *De Orat.* 2. 4. 17 aut se ostentat *aut* eorum quibuscum est *vel* dignitatis *vel* commodi rationem non habet.

See too 34. 7. 8 on *nec dona aut spolia.*

or within a mile's radius of these

=aut propius inde mille passus.

Put what the English *means*, i.e. "or nearer to these than a 1000 paces."

After *inde* we may supply *quam* (cp. *plus semunciam* above).

For *mille passus* acc. of "distance away," see R. § 1088.

More usual than *propius inde* would be *propius urbem*, i.e. the word "city" would be boldly and idiomatically repeated, cp. 40. 44. 6. " In the city and within ten miles' radius of *it*"=in urbe et propius urbem decem milia passuum.

But here *oppida* have to be included and, to avoid the cumbersome *aut propius urbem oppidumve*, Livy writes *inde*=*ab iis*, with his usual love of adverb in place of preposition + demonstrative. See L. and E. p. 53 β.

We say : "nearer to Brindisi"; Latin says : "nearer reckoning from B." Compare Cic. *Att.* 8. 14 "places which are nearer to Brindisi than you are"=loca quae a Brundisio propius absunt quam tu.

for purposes of religious ceremonial

=sacrorum causa.

The genitive is prepositive and has stress—the only exception is in connexion with *religion*.

§ 4.

Note the plural Junii Bruti. We say : "Charles and John Smith"; Latin says : "Charles and John Smith*s*."

and asserted that they would not permit its repeal

=nec eam se abrogari passuros aiebant.

Here "and...not">*nec* i.e. the negative is brought forward.

Note *eam se* ; the normal order would be *se eam*, but "its" has a certain amount of stress, i.e. whatever might happen to other measures, *this one* should not be repealed.

We might expect *negabantque eam se...passuros*, but such expressions as *adfirmabant neque... neque* (3. 12. 3) are more emphatic than *negabant* $\left.\begin{array}{c}neque\\aut\end{array}\right\}\dots\left.\begin{array}{c}neque\\aut\end{array}\right\}$

(W.). Here the emphasis of *aiebant* is shown by its position; for verbs of saying, showing, believing, etc., come early unless emphatic.

its repeal

= eam...abrogari.

English noun > Latin verb.

in support or opposition

= ad suadendum dissuadendumque.

Note *que* = "or," "and as the case might be." So Greek καί preceded by τε, or καί alone.

suadere = "to make something acceptable (*suave*) to someone." Hence *legem suadere, dissuadere* = "to speak for," "speak against a measure." See 34. 2. 12 rogationem...suadent.

and the Capitol

= Capitolium.

There is no connective in Latin. We have three sentences in this paragraph : (1) tribuni...aiebant, (2) nobiles prodibant, (3) Capitolium...complebatur, and, as with a series of nouns, so with a series of sentences (in vivid narrative) Latin either inserts all connectives or omits all, or inserts *que* with the last member.

crowds of people

= turba hominum.

The English plural "crowds" is an odd idiom.

Latin uses *hominum* to include women as well as men.

or condemning

= adversantium*que*. See on *dissuadendumque* above.

measure

=legi.

Just above we have *legem Oppiam*=the Oppian *law*; but English is becoming the slave of variety. This tendency is due to the vast wealth of synonyms which we have acquired from so many languages. English is like Moorish architecture ∶ Latin like some Doric temple, with its repetition of massive simplicity.

§ 5.

Observe how late the subject (married women) comes in English)(Latin. Thus we get in broken English : "The married by no either influence or respect for or order of husbands...were restrained." Latin is formal and without variation—*nec...nec...nec.* Contrast the one "or" of English, and the two words "deaf" and "unmoved," both expressed by the one construction in Latin.

Note *nulla nec...nec.* An original negative may be subdivided by *nec...nec* or *aut...aut.* See also 34. 2. 11 nullam ne privatam quidem rem.

be kept within doors

=contineri limine.

With *contineri* in this sense Livy has (1) *in*+abl., (2) *intra*+ acc., (3) the plain abl. as here. The last is an abl. of means, cp. 34. 2. 10 finibus continere.

They besieged every road

=omnis vias...obsidebant.

The imperfect is frequentative. Note that there is no connective in Latin. It is a case of adversa-

tive asyndeton. The insertion cf
sed is more common when, as here,
the preceding sentence is negatived. But when the first sentence
is positive and the second negative,
then "but not," "and not" must
always be expressed by plain *non*,
e.g. "These are the faults of
character and not of old age"=
haec morum vitia sunt, non senec-
tutis. See M. § 458 (*a*) Obs. 1,
and cp. 34. 2. 14 on "but unless." The form *omnis*=*omnes* is,
normally, used in the accusative
only.

in the city   =urbis.

Only a genitive case can depend on a noun. See below, however, for prepositional phrases
qualifying a noun. Compare Pref.
§ 5. "Reward *for* my labours"=
laboris pretium ; *ib.* § 7. "Renown
in war"=belli gloria ; *ib.* § 11.
"Affection *for* the work"=amor
negotii ; *ib.* § 12. "Passion *for*
wasting oneself"=desiderium per-
eundi ; *ib.* § 13. "Supplications
to gods"=precationibus deorum,
etc. Add 34. 2. 8 verecundia...
maiestatis.

The words *vias urbis* form one
phrase="city-roads" ; hence *urbis*
need not go between *omnis* and
vias, cp. 34. 9. 2 totum orbem muri
(wall-circle) and 34. 9. 6 pars tertia
civium (a third).

and (every) approach to the forum   =aditusque in forum.

The prepositional phrase *in*

forum may qualify *aditus* because this word is of a strong verbal nature and is accompanied by the suitable preposition. So we may say *reditus in urbem, discessio ab urbe*, etc.

It is worth while to formulate the law about prepositional phrases. They must not qualify a noun *standing by itself* unless (*a*) the preposition be (1) *cum, sine* (e.g. " a man without honour " = *homo sine fide*); (2) *in*+acc., *erga, adversus* with nouns denoting a state of mind (e.g. "affection towards you " = *amor erga te*) or a way of acting (e.g. "cruelty towards enemies" = *crudelitas in hostes*); or unless (*b*) the noun be of verbal nature and accompanied by the suitable preposition, e.g. *reditus in urbem, discessio ab urbe*.

But prepositional phrases may always qualify a noun *provided the noun is accompanied by any sort of attribute.*

Thus the following are good Latin : *magnae in Gallia victoriae ; Caesaris in Gallia victoriae.* It would, therefore, be possible to express " every road in the city " by *omnes in urbe vias*, because of the presence of *omnes* ; and *omnes in forum aditus* would be doubly justified under (*a*) and under (*b*).

If no attribute occurs, we must fall back on a relative clause, e.g.

"The man in the garden"=*homo qui in horto est.*

There are phraseological exceptions such as *lex de repetundis (de sicariis,* etc.) and *homo de plebe = homo plebeius.* See M. § 298. 1.

thither   =ad forum, despite *in forum* just preceding—Latin repetition)(English variety. The prepositions are different : *ad,* of course, =towards, while *in*=into.

to remember   This needs no expression in Latin, which merely says: "begging the men, the state being prosperous...to permit."

the prosperity   =florente—English noun > Latin verb.

daily growth of...fortunes   = crescente in dies... fortuna— English adjective>Latin adverb, and English noun>Latin verb. So in Greek : "After the unexpected but signal defeat of the Mede"=τοῦ Μήδου παρὰ λόγον πολλὰ σφαλέντος (Thuc. 6. 33. 6).

Note that *in dies* is, as a rule, associated only with expressions denoting increase or decrease. Otherwise use *cotidie.*

all private fortunes   =privata omnium fortuna.

The plural of *fortuna* is more frequent in this sense.

their wives as well as themselves   =matronis quoque=καὶ ταῖς γυναιξί.

Note English variety—"wives" and "married women" (first word in sentence) and contrast Latin repetition *matronis...matronae.*

§ 6.

The order of the first sentence is abnormal, but so is the event narrated. There was an increasing crowd—of women every day !

A Roman would not be surprised to find the city crowded with *men* at election-time ; but the idea of women crowding the streets would be preposterous. Hence the normal *haec mulierum frequentia* is discarded, and *mulierum* is put outside. Both *augebatur* and *in dies* get stress by reason of their position. There was an *increase* (not a diminution), and this increase went on and on as the days went on and on. All this is lost if we write the normal *haec mulierum frequentia in dies augebatur.* Compare 34. 3. 7 negastis hoc piis precibus earum.

Observe that there is no connective at *augebatur.* Thus from the beginning of § 4 we have had six separate sentences without connectives. This asyndetic short-sentence style is in Livy quite as common as (perhaps more common than) the periodic.

day by day

= in dies.

Above we have "daily"= in dies. Note English variety)(Latin repetition.

as they gathered

= *for* they ... = nam ... conveniebant.

The imperfect is partly "panoramic" (there they were gathering !), partly frequentative.

and villages   = conciliabulisque.

At 29. 37. 3 we have the frequent combination *fora et conciliabula*. The former = "market-towns"; the latter were places of assembly for the inhabitants of several *pagi* in sparsely populated districts. Here courts, religious festivals, levies of troops, markets, etc. were held.

§ 7. And now   = iam.

The word is partly a mere connective = "furthermore"; partly an adverb of time = "already."

consuls, praetors, and other = **et** consules praetores*que* **et** alios
officials   magistratus.

Note the stiff formal grouping of Latin (*a*) major officials, subdivided into (1) consuls, (2) praetors, (*b*) minor officials.

A Roman thinks and writes like an organizer, always arranging and classifying. Here (*a*) and (*b*) = *et...et*, and (1) and (2) = *que*, which performs the same function as *ve* in § 3 *in urbe oppidove*. English dislikes all this marshalling.

But   = ceterum.

A favourite word with Livy. It occurs once in Terence, and once only in Cicero. Sallust first made it popular.

of the first, one   = alterum...consulem.

Latin repeats consul; English varies.

one   = alterum, not *unum*, for "one" = "one of two."

was found

=habebant, "they found." The English varies the subject; Latin retains the same one as long as possible.

and, in support......*he*

=qui.

whose repeal was proposed

=quae abrogabatur.

If we turn this actively—*quam abrogabant*—we see that the tense is a kind of conative imperfect= "which they were trying to repeal, were for repealing." Compare 34. 6. 7 "whose repeal we pro-pose"=quam abrogamus.

Note that the noun "repeal" >verb in Latin. So in the next words : "delivered the following speech"=*ita disseruit*, i.e. the noun "speech">verb, and the adjective "following" > adverb (*ita*).

CHAPTER II

§ 1.   Gentlemen

=Quirites.

Had Cato been addressing the Senate and not the Commons, we should have had *patres conscripti* or *patres* alone. The form of address "Gentlemen" can hardly come later than second or third in our language: here in Latin it comes eighth.

The Englishman usually begins with "Gentlemen," but, in Latin and Greek, such phrases as *Qui-rites, patres conscripti,* ὦ ἄνδρες

'Aθηναῖοι, never come earlier than second in the sentence, and often much later.

So in a preface, e.g.

"My dear Marcus,

Although you ought, etc.,"

we find (*De Off*. 1. 1) quamquam te, Marce fili,...oportet. Compare *ib*. 2. 1 and 3. 1.

each of us =quisque nostrum.

The forms *nostrum, vestrum* (-um=-ων, the old genitive ending) only occur as partitive genitives, while *nostri, vestri*, are exclusively used as objective genitives. Thus "fear of us"=*timor nostri*; "each of us"=*quisque nostrum*.

In English "of us," "of you," etc., are used only as partitive and objective genitives.

in his relations with the mistress of his household =in sua...matre familiae.

Here *in*=in the case of.

Note how *sua* immediately *precedes* quisque, according to the normal order of the idiom.

Livy never uses the old form *familias* (cp. φιλίας) either with *pater* or *mater*—so W.

had from the beginning retained =retinere instituisset.

The verb *instituere* involves three notions: (1) beginning, (2) practising, making an *institution* of, (3) determining.

we should now have =haberemus.

Lit. "we should have been having." It cannot too often be stated that the imperfect subjunctive apodosis expresses an *incomplete* state or action, whether referring to present or past time, e.g. *moreretur*="he would have been dying" (now or then); whereas the pluperfect subjunctive apodosis expresses a *complete* state or action, whether referring to present or past time, e.g. *mortuus esset*="he would have been dead" (now or then).

less trouble

=minus...negotii.

Note the distant separation of this partitive genitive. Such separation is almost the rule, cp. 34. 6. 3 *quid...vani*; 12. 3 *ne quid ...ignominiae*; 14. 5 *quantum... loci*; 29. 6 *quod...muri*; and passim, e.g. 1. 12. 1; 3. 49. 8; 3. 58. 8; 4. 53. 13; 21. 8. 5, etc.

the other sex

=feminis.

"The other sex" is an "ornate alias" for women; therefore in Latin "women" must be written. Latin will have none of the "ornate alias."

as a whole

=universis.

The adjective=an adverb— "collectively." It is prepositive in contrast with *in sua quisque*. If the individual woman had been repressed, collective woman would give less trouble.

§ 2.   Unfortunately

=nunc, i.e. "but as a matter of fact." Like νῦν δέ of Greek, *nunc* may="but as things are" or "but as things were." W. on 1. 28. 9 says that this *nunc* is more frequent in direct and indirect speeches than in narrative. (For νῦν δέ= "but as things *were*," cp. Thuc. 3. 113. 6, and Dem. XXXIV. 15, p. 911. 26.)

ın the home

=domi.

Note how this word gains stress through preceding the subject and so prepares us for the antithesis *in foro*—i.e. a *home* defeat (*domi victa*) means humiliation *outside*. Greek would write : ἰδίᾳ μὲν...δημοσίᾳ δέ.

our liberties

=libertas nostra.

The plural is an English idiom. So "our hopes" will almost always be "*spes nostra.*"

by undisciplined womanhood

=impotentia muliebri.

Lit. "by want of control (ἀκράτεια) belonging to a woman."

have been overthrown...*and*...are being trodden under foot

=victa...obteritur.

In Latin the "and" disappears, because "have been overthrown" becomes a participle.

are being trodden under foot

=obteritur et calcatur.

A rhetorical doublet, like the familiar *oro atque obsecro*, "I hope and pray," "Sin and wickedness," ἀξιῶ καὶ δέομαι.

We have failed to curb...and therefore we tremble

=*et*, quia...non continuimus,... horremus.

Note the connective *et*)(English. Observe how Latin deals with our "and therefore." Thus "I am tired and therefore am going out"=*quia defessus sum*, (± *idcirco*) *exeo*, or *eo* (*idcirco*) *exeo quod defessus sum*. Greek says ἅτε κάμνων ἔξειμι.

Note the matter of fact *non continuimus* "did not curb," for the picturesque English "failed to curb, neglected to curb."

in the mass

=universas.

The same adjective again, despite *universis* ("as a whole") in § 1 above—Latin repetition)(English variety.

§ 3. For my own part

=equidem=ἀλλ' ἔγωγε. Note that *equidem* is almost universally followed by the first person of the verb.

always thought it

=ducebam esse.

W. says that with the active of *ducere* Livy usually omits *esse*.

a fabulous story

=fabulam et fictam rem.

For *rem* see Index.

the whole male population

= virorum omne genus.

Lit. "every class of males." By making *virorum* prepositive, Livy prepares us for the antithesis *muliebri*.

For the story of Lemnos and Hypsipyle see *Classical Dictionary*.

among the women

= muliebri, despite *muliebri* ("womanhood") of § 2 above— Latin repetition)(English variety.

root and branch

=ab stirpe=πρόρριζον.

§ 4. *but* from every class and from both sexes

=ab nullo genere non.

Observe the adversative asyndeton. See 34. 1. 5. (p. 38 at bottom.)

The word *genus* means class or sex ; here both senses are to be understood, but in § 3 (above) only the sense "class" is intended.

cabals, meetings, *and* secret conclaves

=coetus et concilia et secretas consultationes.

Latin either inserts all the connectives (as here) or omits all, or attaches *que* to the last member.

if...are permitted

=si...sinas.

The subjunctive is called that of the "Ideal Second Person," i.e. "you"="one." The passive of English may thus be avoided. Greek, much more often than Latin, evades passive expressions and would here write ἐάν τίς που καὶ ἐάσῃ.

Indeed *I* can scarcely

=atque ego vix.

The insertion of *ego* gives "I" emphasis="I, whatever others may do."

Here *atque* expresses the transition from the general to the particular="and to come to the matter in hand."

which is worse—the proposal itself, or the bad example set in carrying it into effect

=utrum peior ipsa res an peiore exemplo agatur.

Lit. "whether the thing itself (is) worse, or is being done with a worse precedent."

For *res* see Index. Here it means the proposal to repeal the Oppian Law. By *exemplo* is meant the bad precedent set in the behaviour of these Roman suffragettes.

The construction of *peiore exemplo* is ablative of attendant circumstances — "the precedent (being) worse."

§ 5.   Of the two

=quorum.

Note the relative as a connective. Thus *qui* may=*et is* or *sed is.*

the latter

=alterum.

i.e. the women's conduct.

the former

=alterum.

i.e. the proposed repeal.

the proposition before you

=id quod ad vos fertur.

The noun "proposition">verb, *fertur.*

conduces to the common weal

=e re publica sit.

Lit. "in accordance with the public good." Compare *ex animi sententia* = "in accordance with my belief," "to the best of my knowledge and belief." For *re* see Index.

or not

=necne.

In a direct question "or not" is *annon*; in an indirect *necne.*

is a question for you to determine

=vestra existimatio est.

Here *existimatio* = "decision," "appraisement."

We have the verb so used at 31. 48. 5, *de causa existimare* = "to pass judgement on the case."

For *vestra existimatio est qui*, where the relative *qui* has its antecedent in *vestra*, cp. Cic. *Pro Sulla*, 28. 79 and Dr Reid's note. This construction is necessary after such phrases as *mea, tua, nostra, vestra, interest*, cp. Pliny iv. 13. 4 intererat vestra qui patres estis.

The grammars should point out that *sua* (with *interesse, re-*

ferre) can only occur in orat. obl. Thus we may write: *dixit sua interesse*; but "it is to his own interests" must be: *ipsius interest.* = qui in suffragium ituri estis.

who are about to vote

After the *est* (present) of *existimatio est*, another present must occur in the subordinate clause; hence the periphrastic future and not *ibitis* is written.

§ 6.

This is an interesting paragraph and repays careful study. The parenthesis "the blame for it ...shoulders," with its principal verb "rests," is unnecessary in Latin; "rests" can become a participle, and we get—"this agitation...belonging to the fault of officials." Then the dash after the bracket and the repeated "this agitation"+"I say" is merely an English device where a sentence grows too long. All this, therefore, disappears in Latin; for caseendings make lengthy sentences clear both to reader and listener.

Next take the words: "this agitation is...a disgrace; whether a greater disgrace to you...I do not know." Latin can abbreviate this and say: "this agitation... whether it is more disgraceful to you...I do not know."

but this agitation

= haec consternatio—advers. asyndeton.

agitation *by* women

= consternatio muliebris.

The prepositional phrase "by women" can only be expressed by

(1) the genitive *mulierum* (subjective genitive), (2) an adjective,
as here, (3) *a mulieribus facta, nata*
or the like.   See note 34. 1. 5.

a spontaneous effort, it may be, or   =sive sua sponte sive auctoribus
due to the influence of you,   vobis...facta est.

Latin is more formal and pre-
cise.   The noun "effort" > verb
facta est and we get "*whether* of
its own accord *or* you being responsible it was brought about."

Note that *sua* in *sua sponte* is
practically always prepositive ; for
"his own," "their own" etc., necessarily have stress in such a
phrase.

influence   =auctoribus.

English abstract>Latin concrete, cp. 34. 1. 3 *consulibus.*

undoubtedly   =haud dubie (for the normal
Ciceronian *sine dubio*).

Livy uses *haud* freely even
with verbs, provided the verb be
in a principal clause or be a
participle, e.g. *haud ratus.* Cicero
confines the use of *haud* with a
verb to the phrase *haud scio an*
(with sporadic exceptions), and,
in the case of adjectives and adverbs, he avoids *haud* if these
be already negatived or quasi-
negatived.

the blame for it...rests on official   =ad culpam magistratuum per-
shoulders   tinens, lit. "belonging to the fault
of officials."

The phrase "official *shoulders*"
is mere ornamentation for "officials."

whether

=*utrum* understood—Latin often omits *utrum* in indirect questions when *an* occurs.

a greater disgrace

=magis sit deformis.

The adverb *magis* is separated from *deformis*, probably for euphony. Or, perhaps, it is simpler to take *magis*="rather," i.e. "I do not know whether this excitement is disgraceful to you or to the consuls rather."

§ 7.   the shame is yours

=vobis; for "shame" is just ornate variety for "disgrace," and the case-ending of *vobis* makes it easy to supply *est deformis.*

if you have gone the length of bringing

=si...iam adduxistis.

Here *iam*="really," "actually."

it is ours

=nobis.

English here has adversative asyndeton. Greek would write ὑμῖν μὲν...ἡμῖν δέ.

if, like the plebs of old, the women are now to secede and dictate terms

=si ut plebis quondam, sic nunc mulierum secessione leges accipiendae sunt.

Latin expresses the ideas, as usual, with formal preciseness— *ut* is balanced by *sic,* and *quondam* by *nunc.* Then *plebis* (prepositive) is answered by *mulierum* (also prepositive); they are the logical subjects, as if Livy had written: si ut plebs quondam, sic nunc mulieres...leges dicant.

Here *leges* hesitates between the two senses "laws" and "terms." For the phrase cp. 34. 57. 9 neque dicere nec accipere leges=neither to dictate nor submit to terms.

§ 8.   Speaking for myself   = equidem.

not without a blush of shame   = non sine rubore quodam.
                                  The *quodam* = "as it were," "a
                                  kind of (blush)."
a few moments ago   = paulo ante.
                                  English likes a more definite
                                  expression than Latin. Thus "a
                                  minute ago," "five minutes ago,"
                                  "half-an-hour ago" etc. would all
                                  be "paulo ante."
through a crowd of women   = per medium agmen mulierum.
                                  The word *agmen* suggests a
                                  certain orderliness, as of troops on
                                  the march)(*turba*. The women
                                  would be *lining* the streets.
                                  For the order of *mulierum*, see
                                  34. 1. 3 on *in medio ardore belli*.
                                  The *per* in *perveni* implies that
                                  the crowd extended all the way to
                                  the forum.
Had not   = quod nisi, i.e. "*but* if not")(
                                  absence of connective in English.
                                  Note that "but if" = *quod si*,
                                  or *sin*; "but if not" = *quod nisi*, if
                                  the verb is expressed, but *sin minus*,
                                  if the verb is omitted.
Had not respect...prevented me   = quod nisi me verecundia...tenu-
                                  isset.
                                  Observe the order of *me*. It
                                  is, I believe, put forward to make
                                  us feel that it is the real subject,
                                  as if Livy had written *quod nisi
                                  ego verecundiā...tentus essem*. Thus
                                  the abstract subject to a transi-
                                  tive verb with a *personal object* is
                                  not felt to be harsh.
                                  In three other passages only

does Livy use *verecundia* as subject to a transitive verb *with a personal object*, and in two the object is brought forward, viz. 6. 33. 5 inde eos ... verecundia deum arcuisse dicitur; 39. 49. 11 cum alios verecundia ... motura esset; and 24. 42. 9 where, however, the personal object follows the subject.

How instinctively the Roman read such prepositive objects as if they were subjects, may be seen in passages like 5. 6. 8 ut exercitum Romanum non taedium longinquae oppugnationis, non vis hiemis ab urbe...amovere possit nec finem ullum alium belli quam victoriam noverit. Here the change of subject at *noverit* (sc. *exercitus*) would be intolerable but for the fact that *exercitum Romanum* is read as subject at the outset.

For the prepositive object in such cases cp. 34. 12. 1 consulem nocte, quae insecuta est, anceps cura agitare, and for the whole subject see Appendix A.

respect *for*...dignity   = verecundia...maiestatis.

The genitive is objective. Note how English "for" > Latin "of" and compare 34. 1. 5 "every road *in* the city"= omnes vias urbis.

individual dignity   = singularum...maiestatis.

The genitive *singularum* is prepositive because it contains *the* point; Cato respected individuals, but not the whole crowd. This is made still clearer by the separation of *singularum* from *maiestatis.*

(I had no respect for such females collectively)

=magis...quam universarum.

The parenthetic method is not necessary in Latin. It suffices to say: "Had not respect for individuals rather than for the whole mass."

Notice the anticipatory position of *magis* and observe how *maiestatis et pudoris* lies ἀπὸ κοινοῦ between *singularum* and *universarum.*

A double genitive (here *singularum...maiestatis*) should be avoided if any ambiguity is entailed.

§ 9.   What sort of practice is this

=qui hic mos est?

At 6. 7. 3 we have the English order of the demonstrative (qui mos est hic?) but W. there says that the demonstrative between noun and interrogative (as here) is almost invariable in questions expressing astonishment.

The context gives *mos* a bad colour, i.e. = "*bad* habit"; just as in 21. 19. 9 *quae verecundia* = what *want of* modesty. See *iura*, 34. 3. 1.

—running out

=procurrendi.

Note how the dash is translated by a defining genitive.

into the public streets

=in publicum.

Observe the chiastic order: *obsidendi vias et viros...appellandi.*

Latin affects such devices in a series of parallel constructions, cp. Cic. *N. D.* 2. 98 quoted in Postgate's *Sermo Latinus*, p. 52, § 61.

Note also how the three gerundives are connected by *et*, and contrast the one "and" of English. = istud ipsum suos quaeque domi rogare non potuistis?

Could not each of you have made this very request to your own lords and in the home ?

Notice first the pronominal case-relations all grouped together —*istud ipsum suos quaeque.* When a Roman hears these words he has got the gist of the whole sentence. To him it means: "as for this very thing her own people are the proper object (*suos* is objective case) for each woman."

Take a simple instance: *illum tu...accusas?* The Roman, hearing *illum tu*, knows by the case-endings, that "he" (*illum*) is the *object* of "your" (*tu*) action, and he needs no definite verb to make the situation intelligible. Hence the brevity of Roman proverbs, e.g. *sus Minervam* i.e. the pig does something to Minerva, as the case-endings show. English, in a catalogue of pictures, for instance, can say: "Minerva and the pig," but we should have to see the picture before we could tell whether Minerva suffered from the teaching of the pig or *vice versa.*

Sometimes a preposition makes

such brevity possible to English as in "Coals to Newcastle."

For Latin compare Cic. *Phil.* ii. 29. 74 Tam bonus gladiator rudem tam cito? (sc. accipit?), and such instances as Cic. *Off.* 3. 22. 86 *hunc Fabricius* reducendum curavit, and *T. D.* 5. 39. 115 *Polyphemum Homerus*...cum ariete colloquentem fecit.

made this very request
= istud ipsum...rogare.

The English noun "request" > Latin verb *rogare.*

The pronoun *istud* contains a sneer—"this precious request of yours."

§ 10.   Or
= An.

This use of *an* = ἆρα μή, ἆρα οὐ; is common in questions.   Here we can readily supply *utrum* with the preceding question *istud...rogare non potuistis?*

But very often there is no preceding question, and *an* becomes merely a conventional particle with which to introduce a question.

in public
= in publico despite *in publicum* § 9)(variety of English.   For the neuter adjective of 2nd Decl. type = noun, cp. *in privato* below and English "From the blue," "Out of the wet."

to strangers
= *alienis,* despite *alienos* § 9)(variety of English.   The case of *alienis* is dat. of person interested or of person judging.

And yet
= quamquam = καίτοι.

even in the home...it would have been seemly for you to care nothing.

=ne domi quidem vos...curare decuit.

This is a striking instance of the Latin negative brought forward)(the position of the negative in English.

For "it would have been seemly to care"=curare decuit, see Roby § 1520.

if married women were restrained by modesty

=si...matronas contineret pudor.

Observe the order of *matronas*, put early as logical subject. See on 34. 2. 8 nisi me verecundia... tenuisset.

Livy uses the noun *pudor* eleven times as subject to a transitive verb with a *personal* object. In five of these cases *pudor* precedes the object (2. 10. 9; 6. 24. 7; 21, 16. 2; 23. 18. 9; 39. 31. 9); and in six the object (as here) precedes *pudor* (2. 10. 6; 3. 63. 3; 9. 34. 22; 34. 2. 10 and 2. 45. 5 multitudini ...pudor pectora versare et ab intestinis avertere malis, where *multitudini...pectora* = multitudinem). See also Appendix A.

Note *pudor* immediately following the verb. Livy is very fond of a single word (especially an iambus) after the verb, whether of the principal or the subordinate clause.

within the bounds of their due rights

=sui iuris finibus.

Here *sui* (emphatic because prepositive) refers, as commonly, to the *object* of the verb in whose ause it stands. But *matronas* by its position is logical subject and the construction is more easy than usual.

For the construction with *continere* see 34. 1. 5 on *contineri limine*.

it would have been seemly to care = curare decuit.

After the imperfect *contineret* one might have expected *decebat*; but, possibly, Livy is avoiding the verse rhythm— | ārĕ dĕc | ēbăt | at the end of the sentence.

The words *curare decuit* are an analysed form of *curavisses*, i.e. "one should have cared"—the apodosis of *si...contineret*. So *fecisset* ("he would have done") may approach (1) "he could have done" and then be expressed by *facere potuit*, or (2) "he should have done" and then be expressed by *facere debuit, eum facere decuit*.

Similarly, approximate equivalents of *faceret* ("he would have been doing") are *facere poterat* ("could have been doing"), *facere debebat, eum facere decebat* ("should have been doing"). See Roby, Part II. § 1520.

what laws *are* passed = quae leges...rogarentur.

English here could say either "are" or "were"; Latin can only say the latter in view of the past tenses *contineret* and *decuit*. English says: "Then Catiline showed how powerful is (or "was") the influence of conscience," but after the past tense "showed," Latin can say only: *tum...Cati-*

lina..., quanta conscientiae vis esset
(never *sit*), *ostendit* (Cic. *Cat.* 3. 5).
See M. p. 338 § 383.

or rejected
= *abrogarenturve.* Here *ve* is
synonymous with *que.* See 34.
1. 4 on "in support or opposition."

§ 11. Our forefathers..., *but*
we
= maiores nostri... ; nos....
Note the adversative asyndeton
of Latin. Greek would have οἱ
μὲν δὴ πατέρες...ἡμεῖς δέ.

transact...business
= rem agere.
For *res* see Index.

not...any business, even of a private nature
= nullam, *ne* privatam *quidem* rem.
An original negative (here *nullam*) is regularly emphasised by
ne—quidem, where English more
often says "even." See 34. 1. 5
note (p. 38).

without the authority of a guardian
= sine tutore auctore.
i.e. English abstract ("authority") > Latin concrete (*auctore*).
For the sound cp. Cic. *Pro
Sex. Rosc.* § 110 *isto hortatore,
auctore, intercessore.*
It is just possible that in *tutore
auctore* we have an old legal bi-
membral asyndeton, cp. *ruta caesa*
= "minerals and timber." See M.
§ 434.

they were to be
= [feminas...voluerunt...esse] understood. Latin merely supplies
voluerunt with adversative asyndeton i.e. [they wished them to
transact no business...], *but* wished
them etc. Contrast the variety of
English. See 34. 1. 5 note on
"They besieged every road."

of parents, brother, *or* husband

=parentium, fratrum, virorum.

No connectives in Latin)(English and see 34. 1. 4 on "*and* the Capitol."

forsooth

=si diis placet.

This phrase is often equivalent to an exclamation of disgust, cp. English: "but we, *if you please...*!" See Donatus on Ter. *Eun.* 919, and compare Cic. *Pro Sex. Rosc.* § 102. The phrase is frequent in Livy cp. 4. 3. 9; 6. 40. 7; 34. 32. 17; 39. 28. 5, etc.

to appear in the forum

=et foro quoque...(immisceri).

Latin can wait for the verb; English requires one immediately. The combination *et...quoque*= "and...also" appears first in Livy, and is not common. [Neither Caesar nor Sallust has it. It is read by some editors twice in Cicero, and appears once in Plautus. See Draeger, *Hist. Synt.* § 313, p. 33.]

and to join in meetings and elections

=et contionibus et comitiis immisceri.

§ 12. What are they doing... but supporting

=quid...aliud...faciunt, quam... suadent?

Often, in this and similar phrases, the *facere* is omitted, as at 34. 46. 7 nihil aliud quam steterunt parati ad pugnandum=they *did* nothing but draw themselves up in readiness for battle. So in Greek οὐδὲν ἄλλο ἤ=only.

For *suadent* see 34. 1. 4.

of the tribunes

=tribunorum plebi.

For *plebi* see 34. 1. 2.

and voting

= quam...censent.

Latin loves such rhetorical anaphora, cp. 3. 32. 2 "a famine destructive to man and beast alike"=fames...foeda homini, foeda pecori.

§ 13.   free rein

= frenos — from *frenum*, whose plural in prose is *freni*, whereas *frena* is mostly poetical.

that knows no control

=impotenti=Aristotle's ἀκρατής.

The adjectives *impotenti* and *indomito* are prepositive for emphasis; one does not give rein to a fiery and untamed steed.

will set

=facturas.

Note the frequent (in Livy) omission of *esse* with the future infinitive.

At 4. 24. 4 we have *modum imponere.*

extravagance of liberty

=licentiae.

Lit. "doing as you please" (*quodcumque licet*=whatever is open to one).

Observe the repetition of *licentia* in § 14="licence," and 3. 1 = "wilfulness." Contrast the variety of English.

§ 14.   But unless

=nisi=quod nisi.

i.e. an adversative asyndeton. See on 34. 1. 5 "They besieged every road."

you

=vos.

The pronoun is inserted because emphatic.

set such a limit

=facietis.

Latin easily supplies *modum.* Some editors read *feceritis* (fut.

perf.). In any case a future is necessary, for an apodosis in future time must be supplied. In full the sentence would run: "unless you do it yourselves (there will be trouble, for) this is" etc.

of the disabilities = *eorum*.

A loose neuter pronoun or adjective will often translate the more specific expression in English. Compare 34. 3. 1 "with all these restraints" = *quibus omnibus constrictas* and 34. 3. 2 "privileges one by one" = *singula*.

Note the anticipatory position of *eorum* before *est*.

imposed by custom or by law = *aut* moribus aut legibus iniuncta.

Latin almost always inserts the anticipatory "either." English is not so formal. Note that *aut... aut* leaves us no other choice; it is a case of one or the other alternative. But *vel moribus vel legibus* would mean "custom or law or anything else."

under which women chafe = quae iniquo animo feminae... patiuntur.

The words *iniquo animo* (cp. *aequo animo* = with equanimity) are more picturesque than the conventional *aegre, facile, pati, ferre*. They get stress by separation from *patiuntur*: women endure the burden, but under protest—they "kick against the goad."

Liberty in all things = omnium rerum libertatem.

Observe that there is no connective. Cicero would, almost certainly have begun with *denique* = "in fine."

The genitive *omnium rerum*, being prepositive, has stress: *universal* liberty is their aim.

in all things   = omnium rerum.

For genitive of Latin to represent prepositional phrase of English, see on 34. 1. 5 "in the city" = *urbis*.

to speak plain truth   = si vere dicere volumus.

At 41. 23. 13 we find *si vere volumus dicere*, where *vere* separated from its verb *dicere* gains stress and represents "plain truth," "the whole truth and nothing but the truth."

is what they desire   = desiderant.

In such phrases as "It is licence which they desire," "Licence is what they desire," we see a cumbersome English method of expressing emphasis. Latin achieves the same result by order. Here *libertatem ... licentiam* are brought to the front and separated from their verb by *si vere ... volumus.*

CHAPTER III

§ 1.   if they carry this position   = si hoc expugnaverint.

A frequent metaphor. The object of *expugnare* is always some obstacle which you desire to overcome, an enemy whom you desire to dislodge, cp. 1. 58. 5 "He had stormed the citadel of a woman's honour"=expugnato decŏre muliebri; 6. 18. 2 "The plebs conceived hopes of being able to abolish usury"=plebs spem cepit ...faenoris expugnandi; 9. 26. 16 "They used every effort to close the commission" = expugnare quaestiones omni ope adnisi sunt.

and...they will stop at nothing   = quid enim...non temptabunt?

A negative statement may be expressed both in Latin and Greek rhetoric by a question. Thus "No one, surely, would make such an admission"=quis enim fateatur talia? ἀλλὰ τίς ἂν τά γε τοιαῦτα ὁμολογοίη;

Review women's rights and all the limitations....   = recensete omnia muliebria iura.

Note the absence of connective in rhetoric.

Here *iura*="limited rights," just as *mos* in 34. 2. 9="*bad* custom."

by which...and through which   = quibus...per quaeque.

For the "Livian variety" cp. Pref. § 9. "I would have each give his undivided attention to... the deeds of great men, to the qualities in war and peace which won the empire"=ad illa mihi

pro se quisque intendat animum...
per quos viros quibusque artibus
domi militiaeque partum imperium sit ; 2. 24. 5 per metum potius
quam voluntate ; 2. 42. 10 nunc
extis, nunc per aves.

For *per quaeque=et per quae*
cp. 24. 24. 8 singula...quae per
quosque agerentur...ante oculos
posuit, and Cic. *De Off.* 1. 35. 126
ut probemur iis quibuscum apud
quosque vivamus.

Before Livy *que* is never joined
to a preposition, except where the
same preposition has preceded, e.g.
Cic. *Verr.* iv. 61. 115 in religione
inque iis sacris.

they subjected them to their
husbands
=subiecerint viris.

The object *eas* is easily supplied out of *earum* *.

Note *vĭrīs*—a single word after
the verb, preferably an iambus.
This is a favourite Livian order.

and yet with all these restraints
=quibus omnibus constrictas.

Here *quibus=sed tamen his.*
The relative as a connective may
=*et is,* or *sed is, is tamen, sed
tamen is.*

Note that *quibus* is neuter.
Cicero would, preferably, write
quibus rebus, for, with him, the
forms which might be masculine
or neuter are almost always masculine.

The noun "restraints" >verb
constrictas i.e. the abstract idea

* Ussing reads *per quae eas.*

is expressed concretely. For the loose neuter *quibus* representing the specific idea of English, see 34. 2. 14 on "of the disabilities" = *eorum.*

The participle *constrictas* is concessive as *vix tamen* shows.

keep them in check.
= continērĕ pŏtēstĭs.

Observe the hexameter ending. Livy is guilty of it at times.

§ 2. Furthermore
= *quid?* So in Greek rhetoric τί γάρ; τί δέ;

privileges one by one
= singula.

For the loose neuter plural to represent the specific noun of English see on 34. 2. 14 "of the disabilities" = *eorum.*

The word *singula* is in ἀπὸ κοινοῦ position between *carpere* and *extorquere.*

wrest *from you*
= extorquere.

Latin leaves pronominal relations to be understood : English must insert the pronoun.

in the end allowing equality with men
= et aequari ad extremum viris patiemini.

Observe the variety of English. The sentence begins: "if you suffer them to pluck and to wrest," and Latin, with its love of parallel construction, is content to continue: "and (suffer them) to be made equal to men in the end." English, however, would find this monotonous, and shifts to the participle, varying "suffer" by "allowing."

Note how the noun "equality"

think you that you will find them endurable?

> verb *aequari*. This verb is put early for stress.

= tolerabiles vobis eas fore creditis?

The apodosis of *si...patiemini* is *fore*, as if Livy had written *tolerabiles vobis (num sic creditis?) eae erunt?*

Since *creditis* comes last, it probably has stress = "do you *really* believe?"; for verbs of saying, knowing, thinking, showing, etc. come early unless emphatic.

The dative *vobis* is almost the so-called ethical dative. This is a particular case of the dative "of the person interested" i.e. "of the person whose *feelings* are interested." Thus "you will find the whole place ablaze" = tibi ardebunt omnia.

No, the instant they begin

= extemplo, simul...coeperint.

The "No" is translated by adversative asyndeton. The previous question: "think you that you will find them...?" = "You will certainly not find them..."; then "but" is the natural connective, which is here expressed by the asyndeton.

For *extemplo, simul...coeperint, ...erunt*, where *extemplo* has stress by separation from *erunt*, and *simul*, as so often, = *simul ac*, cp. 23. 29. 14 simul...inclinatam... aciem...videre, extemplo...cornua deseruere.

§ 3.   But, we are told

= at hercule.

This is the equivalent of ἀλλὰ νὴ Δία, and more picturesque than *at* or *at enim* in the same meaning.

they take exception to a new measure directed against them

= ne quid novum in eas rogetur recusant.

The adjective *novum* probably has a touch also of "monstrous," "unheard of," as in Horace's *nova monstra*. Remember that *novus* = "never before existent")(*antiquus* = "existent in the past"; while *recens* = "newly existent")(*vetus* = "existent from of old," "long existent."

Livy writes *in eas* not the normal *in se*, because the imaginary speaker, implied in *at hercule*, is giving *his* view of their protest. The independent form is "No new laws are to be made against *them*" not "...made against *us*."

is the object of their protest

= deprecantur.

The words "is the object of" are translated by the objective case, and the noun "protest" > the verb.

Note that *ius* = the whole body of enactments = *leges*.

§ 4.   Nay rather, they demand that

= immo ut....

A simpler form of sentence would be *non ius deprecantur, sed ut...legem abrogetis*. Then after *sed* a verb of positive meaning, e.g. *postulant*, must be supplied out of the negative *deprecantur* = *habere nolunt*. The idiom is com-

mon in Greek e.g. οὐκ ἔφη αὐτὸς
ἀλλ᾽ (sc. ἔφη) ἐκεῖνον στρατηγεῖν.
So English, "No one laughs but
cries on such occasions" i.e. "but
every one cries"; cf. Plato, *Prot.*
323 D οὐδεὶς θυμοῦται...ἀλλὰ (sc.
πάντες) ἐλεοῦσι.

The construction has hardly
received the attention which it
deserves in Latin. A striking
instance is Livy 3. 19. 3 "no one
of whom was inferior to Caeso in
greatness of heart, and *all of
whom* were superior to him because they showed a politic mode-
ration"=quorum nemo Caesoni
cedebat magnitudine animi, consilium et modum adhibendo...pri-
ores erant. Here there is adversative asyndeton before *consilium*,
and we supply *sed omnes* out of the
preceding *nemo*.

An easier case is 3. 48. 1
where after *sed* we supply *dicit*
out of the preceding *negat*.

Other examples are Cic. *De Off.*
3. 2. 9, *De Fin.* 1. 51; Verg. *Aen.*
1. 674, 5; Lucr. 4. 611; Hor.
Sat. 1. 1. 3; Tac. *Hist.* 2. 52 ad
fin., and Livy 3. 37. 3.

that you should repeal a measure =ut quam accepistis...legem,...
which...you have accepted hanc abrogetis.

English prefers the antecedent
before the relative, but Latin
affects, like Greek, the form:
"Who steals my purse, (he) steals
trash," qui crumenam meam furatur, is (hic) furatur scruta, ὅστις

ἂν τὸ ἐμὸν βαλλάντιον κλέψῃ, οὗτος
κλέπτει ῥῶπον.

Here, owing to the lengthy
clauses which intervene, the *ut*
is repeated before *abrogetis*. W.
quotes a large number of examples
at 22. 11. 4.

accepted *and* enacted

=accepistis iussistis.

Note the bi-membral asyndeton, as often in parliamentary and
legal phrases. See M. § 434.

The four consecutive words
ending in *-is* (accepistīs iussistīs
suffragiīs vestrīs) are noticeable.

(a measure) which the use and
experience of so many years have
stamped with your approval

=(legem) quam usu tot annorum
et experiendo comprobastis.

English freely uses abstract
nouns as subjects to transitive
verbs: Latin, or, to be more exact, the Latin of examinations,
avoids the construction (but see
Appendix A) unless the object
also is abstract or non-personal.

The English idiom may almost
always be turned by making the
subject ablative. Thus at 3. 62. 2
"The bravery of the soldiers won
the victory"=virtute militum victoria parta est, where the logical
subject, *virtute*, comes first, while
the grammatical subject, *victoria*,
takes a humble place.

Livy not seldom follows the
English idiom in using an abstract
subject to a transitive verb with a
personal object, but in about 50 per
cent. of the cases he brings forward
the logical subject, cp. *Pref.* § 11 "I

am deceived by affection for the work"=me amor negotii...fallit. See Appendix A.

stamped with your approval   =comprobastis.

The noun "approval" > the verb. The metaphor "stamped with" is dead, and is neither deserving nor capable of reproduction in Latin.

in fact   =id est.

they ask you to...weaken   =ut...infirmetis.

Here "they ask" is mere English variety for the previous "they demand": Latin needs no such device and easily supplies the original verb.

to abolish one law *and so* weaken   =ut unam tollendo legem...infirmetis.

The gerund *tollendo*=a Greek instrumental participle, e.g. ἀπολέσαντες.

Observe how *unam* has stress by separation, thus preparing us for the antithesis *ceteras*. Latin loves such artificial contrasts.

§ 5. But no enactment   =nulla lex.

Observe there is no connective. Note the repetition of *lex*="enactment," after *legem*="measure," and *legem*="law" in § 5. Contrast the variety of English.

acceptable   =satis commoda.

Here *satis*=English "quite."

the only question raised is   =id modo quaeritur.

Note (1) the adversative asyndeton after preceding negative; (2) the anticipatory *id*; (3) how the noun "question" >a verb.

"Does it benefit the majority?"   = si maiori parti...prodest.

Madvig, *Emend. Liv.* p. 495
reads *prosit.* But the indicative
seems to be colloquial, cp. Ter.
Eun. 3. 4. 7 visam si domi est,
and see Roby § 1761. (Compare
also Livy 3. 21. 4 *mirer...si vana
vestra...auctoritas est.*)

Elsewhere, but always with the
subjunctive, Livy uses *si = num*
or *-ne* after verbs of asking, cp.
29. 25. 8 quaesivit si; 33. 35. 3
and 36. 33. 1 percunctatus si; 39.
50. 7 quaesisse si; 40. 49. 6 quaesivit si.

"Is it, in the main, of advantage?"   = et in summam prodest.

Note the variety of English
"does it benefit?" "Is it...of advantage?" Latin is satisfied with
one verb *prodest.*

An individual may be...offended   = si, quod cuique...officiet ius,
by some legislation: is he there-   id destruet..., quid attinebit...?
fore to pull it down...? If so,
what is the good...?

First contrast the separate sentences of English with the formal
subordination of Latin. For instance we write: "I am tired *and
therefore* want to go": Latin says:
*quod defessus sum, idcirco volo dis-
cedere.* An interesting case is 44.
37. 7 "The rising and setting of
sun or moon happened regularly,
and therefore they were not surprised...; *so now,* even though the
light of the latter was withheld...,
they need not count it a miracle"
= itaque QUEMADMODUM, *quia* certi
solis lunaeque et ortus et occasus
sint,...non mirarentur, ITA ne ob-

scurari quidem (lunam)...trahere in prodigium debere.

Next note that there is no connective before *si*. Observe too the relative *quod* picked up by the demonstrative *id*, and see 34. 3. 4 on "that you should repeal a measure which...."

Note also *ius*—a single word after the verb, as so often.

Further, since "is he to pull down" is expressed by the future, therefore the apodosis is future also, and Latin must write "what *will be* the good?"

Lastly English says: "If each is to pull down...the legislation which offends him," i.e. "each" is placed in the principal clause, whereas Latin puts "each" in the subordinate clause. So we say: "Each came down by the nearest path," but Latin says (22. 4. 6) milites qua cuique proximum fuit, decucurrerunt.

what is the good of the community's passing laws = quid attinebit universos rogare leges.

Community = *universos* = *cunctos* = σύμπαντας = all taken together)(the individual = *cuique*.

The verb *rogare* is early to prepare for the antithesis *abrogare*.

which can...be rescinded by those against whom they were directed = quas...abrogare, in quos latae sunt, possint.

The subject of *possint* is the antecedent of *in quos*, as if Livy had written: quas in quos latae sunt ii possint abrogare. But *abrogare* is put early with stress to answer the preceding *rogare*.

Here *quas*=*tales ut* and the consecutive subjunctive follows.

§ 6.   why it is that

=quid sit propter quod.

Lit. "What it is on account of which." The *propter quod*=*tale ut*, "so serious that"—hence the consecutive subjunctive *procucurrerint*.

Compounds of *curro* make the perfect *-curri* or *-cucurri*; but *succurro* makes *succurri* only, and *praecurro* only *praecucurri*.

hysterically

=consternatae.

Greek would write ἐκεῖνο μέντοι βουλοίμην ἂν γιγνώσκειν διὰ τί ἐπτοημέναι ἐς τὰς ὁδοὺς φέρονται αἱ γυναῖκες.

into the public streets

=in publicum.

See on 34. 2. 10. Here *in publicum* is put after the verb for emphasis.

all but invading forum and assembly

=ac vix foro se et contione abstineant.

Note English variety — the change to a participle ; Latin persists with the same form of sentence.

Livy usually omits *a* when *abstinere* is transitive (an exception is 34. 35. 10) and inserts *a* when *abstinere* is intransitive.

Note how *se* is in ἀπὸ κοινοῦ position between *foro* and *contione*.

§ 7.   Is it to redeem

=ut...redimantur.

Latin order groups together

early the important words. The
first thing we hear is *captivi ab
Hannibale*, i.e. "Is it a case of
prisoners of war and Hannibal?"

brothers

=fratres earum.

The point of view is Cato's;
otherwise in a final clause we
should require *sui* (nom. pl.) with
fratres. Compare *eas* in § 3.

Far is and far for ever be

=procul abest absitque semper.

Observe there is no connective.

from our country

=rei publicae.

Like *civitas*, the word suggests
an ordered community: *patria*
would have been merely emotional,
as in "King and country."

Yet, when such misfortune did
come, you refused

=sed tamen, cum fuit, negastis.

Observe *fuit* for the normal
erat. Ordinarily when the principal clause is past, we get in the
subordinate clause (1) past imperfect (imperfect) if the action
or state is contemporaneous with
the action or state of the principal
clause, (2) past perfect (pluperfect)
if the action or state is antecedent
to the action or state of the principal clause.

The great exceptions are (1) the
aorist perfect after *ut* and *ubi*
(=when), *antequam*, *priusquam*,
*postquam, cum primum, ut primum,
simul ac, dum* (=until); (2) the
fact that, when the *cum* clause
follows the principal (*cum = et
eodem tempore*), any tense of the
indicative required by the context
may occur. Thus there is nothing

out of the way in the following nine cases quoted by W. viz. 5. 49. 8, 5. 52. 3, 6. 8. 6, 8. 33. 10, 9. 34. 9, 10. 8. 3, 34. 31. 15, 44. 22. 2, 45. 39. 1.

Livy, however, has a considerable number of instances of the aorist perfect with *cum* = "at the time when" or = *cum primum*. I have noted the following : 1. 41. 7, 2. 40. 7, 2. 51. 1, 3. 14. 4, 4. 44. 10, 4. 60. 8, 6. 20. 4, 21. 39. 4, 23. 20. 5, 23. 49. 5, 29. 37. 8 (Madvig emends), 29. 37. 10, 34. 5. 10, 34. 16. 7, 39. 38. 1, 42. 66. 1, 45. 12. 10 (two cases, one of which Madv. emends), 45. 34. 10. Compare Cic. *De Or.* 2. 59. 242 cum dixit... risimus.

These are genuine cases ; but we must distinguish those where the *cum* clause or relative clause bears no time relation to the principal clause, and is, in fact, a mere date, as it were, or description in a parenthesis, cp. 1. 25. 8, 7. 16. 2, 8. 8. 1, 9. 25. 2, 21. 48. 7, 22. 14. 12, 23. 19. 17, 23. 15. 5, 24. 16. 19, 25. 38. 11, 45. 38. 4, 45. 41. 5.

A few relative clauses are found where the aorist perfect occurs for the normal imperfect or pluperfect, cp. 1. 49. 7 cum quibus voluit,...societates fecit ; 8. 17. 4 quia pestilentia insecuta est...res ad interregnum rediit ; 9. 38. 3 quae superfuit cladi... multitudo ad naves compulsa est (but in 8. 11. 5 we have the normal *superfuerant*); 22. 4. 6 qui ubi, qua cuique proximum fuit, decucurrerunt; 35. 30. 10 Lacedaemonii, quoad lucis superfuit quidquam,... recipiebant se. At 25. 29. 9 the reading is doubtful.

For other anomalies see W. on 1. 1. 1 and Appendix B.

refused this boon

=negastis hoc.

The neuter *hoc* translates the specific noun of English.

to their prayers of love and patriotism

=piis precibus earum.

The words *pius, pietas* etc. used of wives and children imply loyal and dutiful affection; used of the citizen they imply what we call patriotism.

Observe how the sentence is grammatically complete at *negastis*=you refused. The result is that the remaining words gain stress—"*even* this—to *dutiful* prayers—of women like those." The whole is a crescendo. The women of to-day (Cato suggests) make a trivial request; they are neither loyal nor dutiful. Livy writes *piis precibus earum* for the normal *piis earum precibus* in order that *earum* (the women of the past) may re-echo the *earum* of the previous sentence (the women of Cato's day). Compare 34. 1. 6 augebatur haec frequentia mulierum in dies.

§ 8.   But perhaps

=at=at enim=ἀλλὰ νὴ Δία="but it may be said."

it is not love or anxiety = non pietas nec sollicitudo.

Note *non...nec* = οὐ...οὐδέ.

anxiety for their dear ones = sollicitudo pro suis.

For the prepositional phrase qualifying a noun see note on 34. 1. 5 *aditusque in forum.*

it is not love...that has gathered them = non pietas...congregavit eas.

Latin has no such cumbersome method of expressing emphasis as "it is not love...that."

Note the bold personification of *pietas...sollicitudo...religio* made subjects to a transitive verb with a personal object. Livy so uses *religio* 12 times and in 8 of these instances the object is brought forward to occupy the place of the subject. See note on 34. 2. 8 *nisi me verecundia...tenuisset* and Appendix A.

Observe *ĕās*: a single word after the verb, especially an iambus, is a favourite order with Livy.

on Her way = venientem, i.e. the noun > verb.

from Pessinus *in* Phrygia = a Pessinunte *ex* Phrygia.

So "to Rome in Italy" = Romam in Itali*am*.

This cult of Cybele was introduced into Rome in B.C. 205, in obedience to an injunction contained in the Sibylline Books.

No? Then what...? = quid?

The words "No? Then," need no representation in Latin.

what...plea...is put forward to excuse = quid...praetenditur.

The noun "plea" is represented by the neuter pronoun + the verb.

Lit. "What is stretched as a cover in front of."

what honourable plea, honourable at least in word

=quid honestum dictu saltem.

Note the "postpositive" adverb. Thus *saltem* acquires stress, i.e. in word at any rate, if not in deed and fact, λόγῳ μὲν (οὐκ ἔργῳ δέ).

For *dictu* see 34. 1. 1 *parva dictu*. Observe that *honestus* = honourable)(*probus* = honest.

of our women

=muliebri.

Note the emphatic separation from *seditioni* and how *muliebri* comes last—seditioni praetenditur muliebri. Sedition (στάσις) is the business of men (*virilis*), not of women.

Such adjectives as *muliebris, puerilis, virilis, hostilis,* generically used, are common at all periods of Latin, where we say "of *a* woman," "of *a* boy," "of *a* man," "of *an* enemy."

§ 9.   The reply comes

=inquit.

For this *inquit* with obscure subject cp. 6. 40. 8 and *passim*; and compare *aiebat* at 34. 7. 5.

We wish to glitter

=ut...fulgamus.

Weissenborn supplies *procucurrimus* out of § 6. May we not supply *oramus*, or the like, out of *quid...praetenditur*? Note the archaic *fulgĕre*. The ablatives *auro* and *purpura* are ablatives of the means.

every day, festival or no festival

=festis profestisque diebus.

The adjective *profestis* (=nonfestival) is formed on the analogy of *profanus* (=non-sacred, lit. "in front of the *fanum*"=ὅσιος).

to ride...to be carried...   =ut...vectemur.

English requires a verb early and repeats the idea with meaningless variation : one verb suffices in Latin. The word *vectari* is a frequentative of *vehere* and therefore ="be continually carried." So *gerere*="to bear": *gestare*="to wear."

as if in triumph   =velut triumphantes.

The noun of English > verb of Latin. Cicero and Caesar use only *ut* and *quasi* with participles : Livy introduces *velut* and *tamquam* (ὡς, ὥσπερ), as well as *quippe*, *utpote* (ὡς, ἅτε + causal participle), and *quanquam* (καί, καίπερ + concessive participle).

over a law   =de lege.
over your votes   =*et*...suffragiis vestris.

Latin either inserts the connective, as here, or rhetorically repeats the *de*.

taken captive out of your hands   =captis et ereptis.

Note the elaborate chiasmus—de lege victa...et...ereptis suffragiis.

In fine, we ask that no limit should be set   =ne ullus modus...sit.

The more florid rhetoric of Cicero would require : *illud denique oramus et obsecramus ne....*

or to voluptuousness   =ne luxuriae (sit).

Observe the rhetorical repetition of *ne*. In strictness *luxuria* ="tendency to indulgence," while *luxus*="the indulgence itself." See Livy, *Pref.* §§ 11, 12.

CHAPTER IV

§ 1. You have often heard me complain about the expenses of women

= saepe me querentem de feminarum...sumptibus audistis.

Observe the prepositive genitive : its stress tells us that an antithesis (*virorum*) is coming. A Roman would read it as if it ran : "complain about women...and their expenses."

and of men no less

= saepe de virorum...sumptibus.

Note the rhetorical repetition of *saepe de*)(the variety of English : "and...no less."

§ 2. you have often heard me say that...

= ...que.

Latin has another "and" (*que*), but "and's" are growing monotonous in English (we have not the same choice—*et, atque, que*), and a rhetorical repetition of "You have often heard me" with *variety* of "say that" for "complain that" is less tedious to us.

two opposite vices...are endangering the state

= diversis...duobus vitiis...civitatem laborare.

A Roman, in reading this, would scarcely fail to supply *de* with *diversis...vitiis* ; then on reaching *civitatem laborare* he would, as it were, supply the plain causal ablative with *laborare*.

The interesting word is "opposite" (sc. but equally fatal) ; hence *diversis* is prepositive. Livy

6—2

mentions the same two vices in *Pref.* § 11.

curses which

=quae pestes.

Latin draws the antecedent into the relative clause, as regularly in such expressions as "all of whom he killed"=quos omnes necavit.

have proved the ruin of

=everterunt.

The noun of English>verb of Latin. Greek would use the aorist —πολλάκις ἤδη ἀπώλεσαν.

§ 3. And this is what frightens me; for the happier...our country... —the more do I dread the situation, and fear that...

=haec ego, quo melior...fortuna rei publicae est...eo plus horreo, ne....

Here Latin begins with case relations grouped together. (This is especially common with pronouns.)

The words *haec ego* at once tell us that we are concerned with these modern (*haec*) vices (for *haec* cp. *Pref.* § 9, *haec tempora*="these modern days"), that they are the *objects* of ego's solicitous attention. Latin requires nothing more: the verb can wait. English, however, must have a verb at once.

Livy begins as if he were going to write *haec ego...horreo*, but the long parenthesis has suggested new thoughts. Cato's mind is now full of the imperial expansion which has introduced *haec vitia* ; and imperial expansion with its evil consequences (*illae res*) causes the addition of the subordinate clause *ne illae...res nos ceperint.* Thus *haec* acquires a new colour and means "the situation in general." The specific noun of English ("situation") is represented by the loose neuter plural of Latin.

the happier...our country

=quo melior...fortuna rei publicae est.

Lit. "by what measure the fortune of the state is better." The relative *quo* is an ablative of measure of difference and, later on, is picked up by *eo*.

In such phrases we often omit the copula, either in the first clause only (as here) or in both. Latin can omit the copula if it is common to both clauses, e.g. "The more, the merrier"=quo plures, eo hilariores.

The English "the" in such comparative phrases is the old instrumental case of the article.

and the greater the daily increase of our empire

=imperiumque (in dies) crescit.

Thus, as so often, the noun ("increase")>verb, and the adjective ("daily")>adverb.

The comparative idea lurks in *crescit = maius fit*, and Livy's Latin is succinct for *quŏque maius in dies fit imperium*.

In Latin the whole runs more freely with *in dies* in the first sentence, close to the comparatives *melior laetiorque*; then *in dies* is easily supplied with *crescit*.

Remember that *in dies* almost always occurs with comparative notions)(*cotidie*. The phrase *in*

dies = in singulos dies, i.e. for each
day.   Compare *in praesens* (for
the present) and *in singulos annos*
= yearly (Cic. *Att.* 6. 3. 5).

already   = et iam.

We have only one word for
"and": Latin has *et, que, atque,*
and can conceal monotony under
nec and *neve.*   Except for such
monotony, English here could say
"and," in the sense of "indeed."

Asia Minor   = Asiam.

both richly stored with every in-   = omnibus libidinum illecebris re-
centive to voluptuousness   pletas.

Observe that these words *follow*
the verb and thereby have emphasis : the sentence is *construc-*
tionally complete at *transcendimus,*
and anything that follows gains
stress.

every   = omnibus.

Possibly = παντοῖος = *omnis ge-*
neris—a not uncommon sense of
omnis.   So Greek sometimes uses
πᾶς for παντοῖος as in Herodotus
1. 50. 2, 4. 88. 3, and 9. 81. 14.
Compare too 1 *Tim.* 6. 10, ῥίζα γὰρ
πάντων τῶν κακῶν ἐστιν ἡ φιλαρ-
γυρία.

incentive *to* voluptuousness   = libidinum illecebris.

For the genitive, see 34. 1. 5
on "in the city" = urbis.

Note the order (1) adjective
omnibus, (2) complement *libidi-*
num, (3) noun *illecebris.*   The
position of (2) is invariable; but
(1) and (3) may interchange.   Contrast English order.

voluptuousness

=libidinum.

For the plural=instances of luxuriousness, see 34. 1. 1 on *studiis* (p. 29).

nay, our hands covet the treasures of eastern potentates

=et regias etiam adtrectamus gazas.

Note the emphatic order of *regias*, prepositive and separated from its noun.

The words *rex, regnum, regius* are words of abomination to the republican Roman, and suggest the luxurious despots of the East ruling over servile subjects. Observe *gazas*, a single word after the verb. Cicero uses *gaza* in the singular only. The word is Persian.

Draeger, *Hist. Synt.* p. 32, §313, quotes seven instances of *et...etiam* in Livy. This passage should be added. In Cicero *et...etiam* is not infrequent.

the more do I dread the situation, and fear that

=haec ego...eo plus horreo.

Two verbs are necessary in English, but, as explained above, Latin, after the long parenthesis, easily inserts the new subject *res*.

our acquisitions

=illae...res.

For *res* see Index.

have mastered us, not we them

=ne illae magis res nos ceperint quam nos illas.

Observe the anticipatory order of *magis*. So frequently *plus... quam, potius...quam* etc.

Livy uses *res* as subject to a transitive verb with a *personal* object 52 times, with a *non-per-*

sonal object 113 times. See Appendix A.

For the expression cp. Hammerton, *Human Intercourse*, p. 135. "The big English house...masters its master, it possesses its nominal possessor."

§ 4. Believe me   = ...mihi credite.

Livy, like Cicero, writes *mihi crede, mihi credite*, not *crede mihi, credite mihi*.

art treasures   = signa.

I.e. statues, etc. There is a play on *signa inferre* = to advance the standards.

have come like an invading army   = infesta...signa...illata sunt.

Note the stress on *infesta*, prepositive and separated. These are not innocent *signa* (statues) but inimical, ready for hostile action, *signa* that are standards.

The adjective *infestus* is usually employed of things : *infensus* of feelings. Thus *infesto telo* = "with lance in rest"; *infesto agmine* = "in marching order" (as when an army passes through an enemy's territory).

In 1. 7. 6 *ex loco infesto* a place is *infestus*, as we should say "uncanny," "*infested* with dangers."

from Syracuse   = ab Syracusis.

The preposition is normal where, as here, the sense is "from the place and its neighbourhood."

against our city   = huic urbi.

These words, coming last, have

stress. The standards have been advanced and against *us*.

full of praise and admiration

=laudantis mirantisque.

The English nouns>verbs. So below "full of mockery"=ridentis. Note the termination *ī-s* for *-es*, usually for the accusative only.

of Corinth and of Athens

=Corinthi et Athenarum (ornamenta).

Note the prepositive genitives to prepare us for the chiastic antithesis—(*antefixa*)...*deorum Romanorum*, which is put outside *antefixa fictilia* (see 34. 4. 3 on *omnibus libidinum illecebris*) to remind us of *Corinthi et Athenarum*.

on the temple pediments

=antefixa (sc. *tectis templorum* or the like).

Latin often uses participles with the indirect object to be supplied.

The word *antefixus* only occurs as a participle.

§ 5. . But, for myself, I prefer these gods and their blessing

=ego hos malo propitios deos.

Observe the crowding of case-relations early—*ego hos* (cp. *ego haec* in the previous section). Indeed the sentence is constructionally complete at *malo*, and thus the prepositive *propitios* gets a double stress. The resulting effect is: "I prefer these, because they bring blessing (and not harm) and because they are gods (not mere works of art)."

Note that *ego* is inserted="*I*, whatever others may do."

The word *propitius* is derived

from the art of the *auspices*. Its root is $pro + \pi\acute{\epsilon}\tau\epsilon\sigma\theta\alpha\iota$ = "belonging to a forward-flying bird"; hence "favourable as an omen."

and I trust that they will grant it, if only

= et ita spero futuros (sc. propitios) si....

Observe *ita* anticipatory of *si* = "on this condition...namely if."

we suffer

= patiemur.

The principal clause is future; therefore the subordinate clause must be future also—simple future (as here) if the action of the clauses be contemporaneous: perfect future, if the action of the subordinate clause is antecedent to that of the principal clause.

to remain in their old homes

= in suis manere sedibus.

Note the stress on *suis* prepositive and separated from its noun. Here *suis* refers to the subject of *manere* (i.e. *eos* understood) or, if we care to put it so, to the object of *patiemur*, viz. *eos*. Compare 4. 33. 5 suis flammis delete Fidenas.

§ 6. Within the memory of our fathers

= patrum nostrorum memoria, i.e. in B.C. 280. The genitive precedes because *patrum* is practically subject, as if "our fathers remember how...."

The ablative *memoria* is quasi-temporal, equivalent to "in the time of."

the envoy Cineas was employed by Pyrrhus in an attempt

= per legatum Cineam Pyrrhus... temptavit.

Here *per* expresses the agent,

cp. δι' ἀγγέλου. Cineas was sent
to Rome B.C. 280.

in an attempt to bribe

=...donis temptavit.

The noun "attempt" > verb.
For the phrase cp. χρήμασι, δώροις
ἔπειθε (conative imperfect = *tried*
to win over by bribes).

not only men but women also

=non virorum modo sed etiam
mulierum animos.

Note the insertion of *animos*.
This word is extremely common
in Latin, but foreign to our idiom.
Compare *Pref.* § 5 "to divert a
writer from the path of truth" =
scribentis *animum*...flectere a vero,
where, as here, the genitive precedes, because the person is really
meant, not merely his mind.

The Oppian law had not yet been
passed

=nondum lex Oppia...lata erat.

Observe the adverb *nondum*
put first with great emphasis : its
normal position would be immediately before *lata erat*.

for all that, not one woman

=tamen nulla.

The conjunction *tamen* comes
first, if qualifying the whole sentence, but second, if qualifying a
single word.

Note that *nulla* provides a
feminine for *nemo*, cp. 34. 7. 5.

accepted a bribe

=accepit.

The object *dona* is readily supplied. Compare on *antefixa* § 5
above.

§ 7. And what, think you,
was the reason ?

=quam causam fuisse censetis ?

Latin omits "and," and does
not make "think you" parenthetic.
In the *first person* such paren-

The same reason which

thetic expressions as *inquam, credo, ut opinor*, etc. are common enough. =eadem fuit quae....

Latin repeats the verb, as in answering any question, e.g. "Are you coming?" "Yes"=venisne? venio.

which led our ancestors to make no legal provision in the matter

=quae maioribus nostris nihil de hac re lege sanciundi.

Lit. "(the reason) which was (*fuit* is readily supplied) to our ancestors of enacting *nothing* (emphatic by separation from *sanciundi*) by law."

The personification "a reason which led our ancestors" is not too bold for Livy; for at 10. 18. 11 we have *quae te causa, ut provincia tua excederes, induxit?*

We say "reason *for* enacting": Latin says "reason *of* enacting." See 34. 1. 5 on "in the city"=*urbis.*

make...legal provision

=lege sanciundi.

The adjective "legal">quasi-adverb *lege*, and the noun "provision">verb *sanciundi*. Note the archaic gerund form *-iundi*, for *-iendi*. This is mainly confined to verbs in *-io*.

there existed no luxuriousness

=nulla erat luxuria.

There is stress on *nulla* by separation. The adjective *nullus* is equal to a strong negative, as often in Cicero.

The imperfect *erat* expresses a continuous state. Above we have *fuit* with *eadem*, where the reference is to a single event.

(luxuriousness) to be curbed

= quae coerceretur.

The subjunctive is allied to the jussive (future in the past). In primary time we can say: nulla est luxuria quae coerceatur = "which is to be, must be, ought to be curbed." So *faciat* = "he is to do" = "he ought to do," "he should do."

§ 8.   before we can know the remedy

= ante...quam remedia eorum (sc. cognita esse).

Note the anticipatory order of *ante*; and observe that Latin supplies the same verb. Contrast the variety of English—"diagnose"—"can know."

come into existence

= natae sunt.

This is a present perfect— γεγόνασι not γίγνονται, "are in existence" not "are coming into existence (*nascuntur*)." Here Livy follows Cicero's practice of preferring past consecution *facerent* after any sort of perfect.

before the laws which are to limit them

= prius...quam leges quae iis modum facerent.

Notice again the anticipatory order of *prius*, like *ante* above. Also observe the Livian variety *prius* for *ante*, and *iis modum facerent* for *eas coercerent*.

are to limit

= modum facerent.

Thus "are to limit" > "were to limit," because, as above pointed out, *natae sunt*, though a perfect present, is followed, according to Cicero's usage, by a past consecu-

§ 9. What called forth the Licinian law

tion. For *lex* as subject to a transitive verb, see 4. 13.

= quid legem Liciniam evocavit... ?

This law was carried B.C. 367, and one of its provisions was that no citizen should occupy more than 500 iugera of public land.

with its restriction of 500 acres

= de quingentis iugeribus.

These words come as an afterthought: the sentence is constructionally complete at *excitavit*. The effect is like: "What called forth the Licinian law—I mean touching 500 acres?"; for the Lex Licinia had many other provisions.

inordinate

= ingens.

passion *for* enlarging estates

= cupido agros continuandi.

For "passion *for*" = "passion of" see 34. 1. 5 on "in the city" = *urbis*.

Livy has *cupido* ten times subject to a transitive verb. The object is personal in seven of these ten cases. See Appendix A.

Cicero uses *cupido* only in the sense of Cupid. He would write *cupiditas, desiderium, studium*.

Note the order: the object *agros* between the noun *cupido* and the gerund. This is normal.

Just as *continui montes* = "an unbroken chain of mountains," so *agros continuare* = "to form an unbroken series of estates." These estates were called *latifundia* and were worked by slave-gangs. Thus the small owner was driven out of the country into the towns.

against gifts and presents   =de donis et muneribus.

The Lex Cincia of B.C. 204 forbade *patroni* to accept fees or gifts for defending their *clientes* in the courts.

pensioners and dependents   =vectigalis iam et stipendiaria.

The adjectives are prepositive because predicative and emphatic.

Note the ἀπὸ κοινοῦ position of *iam*.

the plebs had...commenced to be...   =plebs esse senatui coeperat.
(dependents) of the senate

Note the separation of *esse* from *coeperat*: it helps to emphasise the antithesis *plebs* and *senatus*.

Properly speaking *coepi* is a perfect present="I have begun")(*incipio*="I am beginning," but it is also used as an (Aorist) perfect="I began."

§ 10.   Observe *itaque*—the first formal connective in this chapter. Such want of connectives is frequent in rhetoric, but not in narrative, save in the very short sentence style.

any other   =aliam ullam.

Unusual for *ullam aliam. Ullus* is the adjective of *quisquam* and provides its feminine.

any other law was wanted   =aliam ullam tum legem desideratam esse.

Note the anticipatory *tum* (anticipating *cum* of *cum...accipiebant*) and its emphatic position. No law was wanted *in those days*.

to limit   =quae modum...faceret.

The relative *quae*=*ut* (in order

that)+*eā*. For *lex* subject to a
transitive verb see 34. 4. 13.

when
=cum. For this *cum*="in that"
=*quod* with the indicative, cp.
21. 18. 4 praeceps vestra...et prior
legatio fuit, cum Hannibalem...
deposcebatis="Your previous em-
bassy showed no less hastiness *in
demanding* Hannibal for punish-
ment."

refused to accept
=non accipiebant.

Lit. "were not for accepting"
—a conative imperfect. Greek, as
so often with a negative would
here use the imperfect cp. οὐκ εἴα,
οὐκ ἠξίου, οὐκ ἔθελε, οὐκ ἔπειθε κ.τ.λ.

freely given, nay thrust upon them
=data et oblata ultro.

The *et* seems to be corrective
or explanatory="given, *that is to
say*, offered freely." For this *et*
see W. on 3. 1. 3 possessores et
magna pars patrum.

It is just possible that *data*
might = "given at the request
of husbands," who were thus in-
directly bribed. Contrast *oblatum*
="freely offered without sugges-
tion (*ultro*)." Compare Cic. *Verr.*
1. 1. 1 divinitus datum atque
oblatum="given by heaven (in
answer to our prayers), nay thrust
upon us (whether we wished it or
not)."

For the emphatic postpositive
ultro cp. 1. 17. 8 offerendum ultro
rati; and for *ultro* emphatic by
separation cp. 40. 23. 1 in omnia
ultro suam obferens operam.

The neuter *data* referring to *aurum et purpuram* is normal. See M. § 214 b.

§ 11.   But, to-day, if

= si nunc.

The adversative asyndeton is more emphatic than the normal *quodsi, sin.*

had Cineas gone the round of the city with his bribes

= si...cum illis donis Cineas urbem circumiret.

The imperfect *circumiret* = "had been going round")(*circumisset* = "had gone round."

The words *cum illis donis* are brought to the front because the bribes are more important than the briber : they go the rounds quite as much as Cineas and are practically subject.

in the public streets

= in publico.

See 34. 2. 10 on *in publico*. It is ἀπὸ κοινοῦ with *stantis* and *invenisset*.

to receive them

= quae acciperent.

quae = *ut* (in order that) *eae.*

§ 12.   Indeed

= atque = yes and.

I cannot find even the ground

= ego...ne causam quidem...inire possum.

Note *ego* inserted for emphasis = ἔγωγε or ἐγὼ μέν, whatever others may do.

Latin writes : "not even the ground can I find," i.e. the negative is brought forward. So "even then he did not deceive the enemy" = ne tum quidem fefellit hostes.

ground *for* desires

= cupiditatium...causam.

See 34. 1. 5 "in the city " = urbis.

or the motive

= aut rationem.

Here *ratio* = origin, rationale. The phrase *rationem inire* = "to give an account of, to account for" is not uncommon, but with *causam* we should expect *invenire*.

The use of *aut* to carry on a preceding negative is found first in Cicero, but becomes more common later, cp. Liv. 3. 16. 4 nemo tribunos aut plebem timebat. (Gild. and Lodge, § 493. 3.)

Granting that...still

= nam ut (+ subjunctive concessive)...sic.

Note the connective.

the denial of what is lawful for one's neighbour

= quod alii liceat, tibi non licere.

Here *tibi* is the ideal second person = "one" = τινί.

The phrase *non licere* = τὸ μὴ ἐξεῖναι = "the fact that it is not lawful." Out of *quod* we supply *id* as subject to *licere*: lit. "what is lawful for another, the fact that this (*id* accusative) is not lawful for one (*tibi*) brings vexation."

The subjunctive *liceat* is due to attraction; it stands within a subjunctive clause *ut...habeat*.

brings with it some...feeling of... vexation

= aliquid...indignationis habeat = ἀγανάκτησιν ἔχει (where ἔχει = "involves").

The infinitive *non licere* is here subject to a *transitive* verb. This is rare. There are in Livy five cases with *fallere* (always accompanied by a negative), e.g. 31. 33. 8 neutros fallit...hostes appropinquare.   Add 5. 2. 3; 30. 31. 1; 33. 47. 9; 40. 21. 7. [Compare 31. 25. 8 non fefellit Achaeos quo spectasset tam benigna pollicitatio.]

Less striking is 45. 5. 11 subiit extemplo animum, in se nimirum receptam labem, quae Evandri fuisset; but 40. 21. 8 *ne invitum (se) pārēre* (τὸ ἄκων γε πείθεσθαι) *suspicionem faceret* is very bold.

Other concealed infinitives, subjects to *transitive* verbs, are *auditum* 27. 45. 4; 28. 26. 7; *pronuntiatum* 4. 59. 7; *nuntiatum* 27. 37. 5; *temptatum* 7. 22. 1; *non perlitatum* 7. 8. 5; *cautum* 4. 16. 4.

Very similar are such cases as 1. 55. 4 non motam Termini sedem...firma cuncta portendere, and 30. 38. 12 laetitiam populo... addidit sedes sua sollemni spectaculo reddita, etc.

feeling of shame	= pudoris.
feeling of vexation	= indignationis.
some...feeling of shame or vexation	= aliquid aut pudoris aut indignationis.

Note the anticipatory *aut* before *pudoris*)(the one "or" of English.

when fashions are the same for all	= aequato omnium cultu.

Note the normal order: attribute (*aequato*), complement (*omnium*), noun (*cultu*). The first and third may interchange.

wherein need each one of you ladies fear to be made conspicuous?	= quid unaquaeque vestrum veretur ne in se conspiciatur?

Lit. "What does each...fear lest it may be seen conspicuously in her case ?" For *vestrum* see 34. 2. 1 on *quisque nostrum.*

Evidently the meeting is in the open forum, and the ladies are listeners.

§ 13.   The lowest shame

= pessimus quidem pudor.

Observe *quidem* = μέν answered by *sed* = δέ.

Livy is perhaps the first to represent μέν regularly in this way, attaching the *quidem* to *any part of speech.*

Pre-Livian Latin expressed antitheses by order and asyndeton, e.g. "The citizens left, but the soldiers remained" = *cives abeunt, milites manent* or (by chiasmus) *manent milites*; but Livy would also write: *cives quidem abeunt, milites autem (milites vero, sed milites) manent.*

Cicero does, at times, use *quidem* with the first clause, but always attaches the *quidem* to a pronoun. Here he might write *pessimus ille quidem pudor est.* See M. § 489 b.

is shame of thrift or humble circumstances

= est (sc. pudor) vel parsimoniae vel paupertatis.

Note the anticipatory *vel* before *paupertatis*)(the one "or" of English.

The word *paupertas* merely = restricted means)(*egestas* = poverty.

both forms of shame

=utrumque.

The neuter is used referring to two inanimate things. The plural *utraque* would mean "each of two *sets* of things."

Note the emphatic position of *utrumque*—the object before the subject.

Livy has *lex* subject to a transitive verb 29 times. In 26 of these cases the object is expressed. In 9 only is the object personal. Compare 34. 4. 8, 4. 10, 4. 18, 6. 10, 7. 11. See Appendix A.

when

=cum, with the indicative, as always when the *cum* clause follows the principal. Here *cum* nearly=*quod*=in that.

Cicero confines this *cum* (=in that) to present tenses. Both he and Livy use *dum* in much the same way.

For *cum* cp. 34. 4. 17 *cum... videbit.* See also W. on Liv. 8. 33. 10.

§ 14. "But," says our wealthy lady, " it is just this...that "

="hanc" inquit "ipsam..." illa locuples.

The position of *illa locuples* is so strange that one is tempted to bracket it as a gloss. The subject of *inquit* may be vague as at 34. 3. 9.

Such an expression as " It is just this equality which..." is merely an English idiom by which to stress "this." Latin achieves the effect by *order*, and puts *hanc* first, separating it from *ipsam* by *inquit*.

Why may I not attract attention...?
= cur non...conspicior ?

Observe the position of *non*. The order *cur insignis auro...non conspicior ?* would mean: "Why, when I am a blaze of gold,...am I not to be looked at ?" The negative in Livy's order does, as it were, double duty, as if " Why am I not a blaze of gold, and therefore not looked at ? "

In indignant questions, we often have the indicative, rather than the deliberative subjunctive. See Roby § 1611, and contrast § 1610.

by a blaze of gold
= insignis (sc. οὖσα) auro.

Lit. "(being) distinguished by gold."

Why should the poor circumstances...find concealment ?
= cur paupertas...latet ?

For the indicative cp. *conspicior* above; and for *paupertas* see on 34. 4. 13.

under this pretext of a law
= sub hac legis specie.

For order see 34. 4. 12 aequato omnium cultu. Probably *hac* = *tali*.

making it seem that...they might have had
= ut...habiturae...fuisse videantur.

Lit. "so that they seem to have been going to have."

This is a somewhat complicated piece of syntax. First take a simple instance : " If he had been doing this, he would have been doing well "= *si hoc faceret, bene faceret* or *bene facturus erat.*

If we put this latter apodosis in
Or. Obl. (e.g. after *dixit*), we get
eum...bene facturum fuisse (for
an imperfect—here *erat*—becomes
perfect infinitive). Thus in Or.
Obl. there is no distinction between *dixisset* and *diceret* of the
recta : both become *dicturum
fuisse*.

Next take such a phrase as :
" it seems that you are wrong."
Latin turns this personally, i.e.
videris errare, and therefore "it
seems that you would have been
wrong"=*erraturus fuisse videris*,
where *errares* of the independent
form becomes *erraturus fuisse*
when dependent and infinitive.
Thus " it seems that they might
have been having " becomes "ha-
biturae...fuisse videntur."

what they cannot afford
=quod habere non possunt.

Here *non possunt*="have not
the means"; hence "afford" may
be represented by *habere*. Note
Latin repetition *habere...habiturae*
)(English variety " afford "...
" have had."

but for legislation
=si liceret.

The noun of English > verb of
Latin. Lit. " if it had been being
lawful."

§ 15.   Gentlemen
=Quirites.

See note on 34. 2. 1 and contrast the position of *Quirites* with
that of "Gentlemen."

such rivalry...as will cause the
rich to desire
=hoc certamen...ut divites...ha-
bere velint.

Here *hoc* = *tale*, and *velint* is consecutive subjunctive.

only what no one else of their sex can have

= id...quod nulla alia possit.

Observe the anticipatory order of *id*, translating "only."

The phrase "no one else of their sex" is mere variety for "no other woman." Put what the English *means* in its simplest form. The feminine gender translates "woman."

The word "have" in "can have" may readily be supplied from the previous *habere*.

and the poor

= pauperes.

Latin uses asyndeton.

Greek would have αἱ μὲν πλούσιαι...αἱ δὲ πένητες.

fearing contempt

= ne...contemnantur.

The noun "contempt" > verb. The verb *contemnere* = ὀλιγωρεῖν = think lightly of, and is not so strong as *despicere* = καταφρονεῖν = despise.

on this very ground

= ob hoc ipsum.

The specific noun "ground" is expressed partly by the loose neuter of Latin, partly by the preposition.

to overstrain their means

= supra vires se extendant.

The metaphor is purely physical in Latin.

§ 16.   Assuredly

= nē = ναί.

This *ne* always seems to occur along with some pronoun, e.g. nē ego, nē tu, nē ille, etc. This is one reason for inserting *eas*.

so soon as

= simul = simul ac, as so often.

they feel shame...they will cease to feel it

=eas simul pudere...coeperit,... non pudebit.

Note the emphatic position of *eas*; the sentiment, Livy hints, is peculiarly true of women.

The periphrasis *pudere...coeperit* provides a future perfect for *pudet*.

where shame should not exist

=quod non oportet (sc. *pudere*).

The antecedent of *quod* is *id* understood, and the construction is: *simul (ac) id quod non oportet (pudere), eas pudere coeperit.* This personal use of *pudere* is only found elsewhere in Comedy, e.g. Plaut. *Mil.* 3. 1. 30 si quidem te quicquam, quod facis, pudet, and Ter. *Ad.* 1. 2. 4, etc.

The present tenses *non oportet* and *oportet* may stand in a clause which is future, because *oportet*= is, will be, and would be right. So *longum est*=is, will be, and would be a long story. Compare *par est, facile est, difficile est*, etc., and δεῖ, χρή=it is and would be necessary, right.

who possesses the means

=quae de suo poterit (sc. parare).

Lit. "who is able (to get it) from her own (income)." We say "*is* able," but Latin must have future in the subordinate clause if the principal clause is future.

So below "who does not" > quae non poterit.

§ 17.   Unhappy man

=miserum illum virum.

This is the accusative of exclamation. The *illum* is anticipatory of *et qui...et qui.*

whether he yield to her prayers or not !

= et qui exoratus et qui non exoratus erit.

Observe the formal precision of Latin : "both one who in the future is won over and one who in the future is not won over." To us the *et...et* and the repeated *exoratus* are intolerable.

I have kept the English subjunctive "yield"; but modern idiom would permit the careless syntax of "yields"—a present tense, despite the fact that the reference is to the future. Contrast the accuracy of Latin.

what he does not give himself... he will see

= cum, quod ipse non dederit,... videbit.

Note the connective *cum,* which here = ἐπεί in the sense of γάρ = *nam,...enim.*

For *cum* = "seeing that," "in that," with the indicative, see note on 34. 4. 13 *ad fin.*

does not give

= non dederit.

Future because the principal clause is future ; and future perfect because the action of *dederit* is antecedent to, not contemporaneous with, *videbit.*

he will see given by another

= datum ab alio videbit.

The normal order would be *ab alio datum,* but *datum* is brought close to *non dederit* to point the antithesis, and *ab alio* comes as an after-thought, i.e. "given, not refused—and by another !"

§ 18.   Even now

husbands of others

what is more
they ask for a measure

and get them, too,

in certain quarters

But it is to the detriment of
yourself, Sir,...that you are compliant

=nunc.

The adverb is emphatic; they
may do worse in the future.

=alienos viros.

There is stress on the prepositive *alienos*. It is not their own
husbands only whom they solicit.

=quod maius est.
=legem...rogant.

There is a reference to the
technical *legem rogare*= " to introduce a bill." As a matter of fact
they are only asking the *repeal* of
a *lex*.

Note the Latin repetition—
rogant...rogant)(English variety
—"solicit"..."ask for."

=et...impetrant.

The verb= "to ask and get."

=a quibusdam.

The English *means* "from certain persons"; hence the Latin
version.

=adversus te...exorabilis es.

Note the adversative asyndeton. The speaker apostrophises
an imaginary husband. The
"Sir" needs no representation in
Latin.

Observe the cumbersome English method of emphasising "to the
detriment of yourself," viz. "it is
to the detriment of yourself...that
you are." Latin achieves the result by order.

The adjective *exorabilis* (= παραιτητός) re-echoes the *exoratus* of
§ 17.

your property and your children = *et* rem tuam *et* liberos tuos.

Latin (1) omits all connectives; (2) inserts all (as here); (3) attaches *que* to the last member.

The word *liberi* refers to the children of a definite person. Contrast *pueri*=children, as a class. So *libertini*=freedmen, as a class, but *liberti*=the freedmen of a definite person.

once let the law cease to limit... and *you* will never succeed in doing it = simul lex modum...facere desierit, tu numquam facies.

Again *simul*=*simul ac*. We say: "as soon as the law *ceases*," but, in Latin, the time of the subordinate clause must be future, because the principal clause is future, and the tense must be future perfect, because the "ceasing" is antecedent to the time of *facies*.

you = tu.

Since "you" is emphatic, the pronoun must be inserted.

will never succeed in doing it = numquam facies (sc. modum).

Note the repetition *facere... facies*, and contrast the variety of English.

§ 19.   Do not imagine = nolite...existimare.

This is the most common way of expressing a prohibition; *ne* + perf. subj. is comparatively rare.

that the position will be the same = eodem loco...futuram rem.

Lit. "that the thing will be in the same position." Livy uses *loco ± in*, whether literal or metaphorical.

The *esse* is omitted, as so often with the future participle.

Note the great emphasis on *eodem loco*, by separation from *futuram*.

For *rem* see Index.

before the law was passed

= antequam lex...ferretur.

There should be a notion of purpose prevented to account for the subjunctive, i.e. "before the law could be passed," but Livy, not seldom, has the subjunctive with *antequam, priusquam*, etc., apparently on the analogy of *cum* expressing attendant circumstances.

to deal with it

= de hoc = de hac re. This latter Cicero would write because he uses the ambiguous forms only as masculine. Livy often combines a neuter with a preceding *res*. See W. on 32. 10. 3.

It is less dangerous

= ...tutius est.

for a bad man to escape trial

= et hominem improbum non accusari (tutius est).

Observe the *et* before *hominem*. It anticipates the *et* before *luxuria*, and nearly = *ut...ita*, μέν... δέ. The thought is: a bad man has tasted prison when awaiting trial; if acquitted, he is more dangerous, because resentful. It is the same with a bad habit: there is less danger in leaving it unrestricted, than in restricting it first and then allowing it free play again. It then becomes like a wild beast, released suddenly from galling chains.

The subject of *est* is τò—hominem—non—accusari, i.e. "the fact that a man is not brought to trial."

would have been

= esset.

Lit. "would have been being."

than it will be now

= quam erit nunc)(quam nunc erit.

By putting *erit* first Livy brings out the antithesis to "what might have been (*esset*)," and also gives stress to *nunc*.

maddened, like some wild beast, by its very chains

= ipsis vinculis, sicut ferae bestiae, irritata.

Observe the order of Latin. Too many beginners would write *irritata* first. But a Latin phrase, like a Latin sentence, if constructionally complete, is *ipso facto* at an end. In the beginner's order, *irritata, sicut ferae bestiae, ipsis vinculis*, the phrase *should* finish at *irritata*, and then again at *bestiae*, but it does not.

like some wild beast

= sicut ferae bestiae.

Latin has the plural (Livy thinks of the beasts in the amphitheatre), but the singular is more natural in English, parallel to the singular of *luxuria*.

The adjective "wild" has stress; hence *ferae* is prepositive.

and then

= deinde, never *et deinde*.

§ 20.   I therefore move

= ego...censeo.

This is the usual formula employed, in concluding a speech, by the mover of a resolution.

Compare 10. 8. 12 ego hanc legem
...iubendam censeo. Note the
absence of connective and the
omission of *esse* in both passages.
For the inserted *ego* see below.

but   =adversative asyndeton.

The pronoun *vos* is inserted to
form an artificial antithesis to
ego = ἐγὼ μέν...ὑμεῖς δέ, i.e. I
propose one thing: you may
do another, but whatever you do
may it have heaven's blessing.

whatever course you adopt   =quod faxitis.

The specific noun "course"
>the indefinite neuter of Latin.

The form *faxitis* is from *faxo*,
an archaic future of *facere*, cp.
τάξω. Such archaisms may be
expected in an old parliamentary
formula.

The future is used in the subordinate clause, because the principal clause, being an expression
of wish that something may
happen, has necessarily a future
sense.

may the blessing of every god rest   =deos omnis fortunare velim.
upon it
The noun "blessing" > the
verb *fortunare*.

Here *velim* = βουλοίμην ἄν.
Such an apodosis, when the protasis is regularly suppressed, we
call "potential subjunctive." The
apodosis *velim* is really a remoter
future, i.e. "I should wish, (if it
were to be of use)." Contrast
cerneres, videres = "you might have
seen"; lit. "you would have been

seeing (if you had been present)."

For *omnis=omnes* cp. on 34. 4. 4 *laudantis*.

Throughout this chapter note the absence of connectives. In § 10 we have *itaque*, in § 12 *atque* and *nam*, and in § 13 *sed*, but no others.

CHAPTER V

§ 1.   After this speech

=post haec.

Again the indefinite neuter of Latin represents the specific noun of English.

those plebeian tribunes

=tribuni quoque plebi.

The force of *quoque* is merely "on the other hand"; like the Greek καί in μετὰ δὲ ταῦτα καὶ οἱ ἄλλοι.

Note the archaic *plebi* for *plebis* and see on 34. 1. 2.

who had promised their intervention

=qui se intercessuros professi erant.

The noun "intervention">the verb of Latin. There is the usual omission of *esse* with a future participle.

added a few words to the same purport

=cum pauca in eandem sententiam adiecissent.

With *pauca* supply (perhaps) *verba*. The *in* with *sententiam* is like the *in* of such phrases as *in*

bonam (malam) partem accipere
="to take something in good
part."

Note that Latin subordinates
"added" in a *cum* clause, and
picks up with *tum.*

addressed the assembly =ita disseruit.

in support of the bill =pro rogatione.

which he himself had brought =ab se promulgata.

forward

Observe the order: "the bill
brought forward by himself"=
rogatione ab se promulgata. The
position of the complement (*ab se*)
is invariable. Usually the attribute comes first, but *pro promulgata* would sound too ugly.

See on 34. 4. 12 aequato omnium cultu.

The word *promulgare* pro-
perly=to placard, post up, so
that the people may know the
terms of the proposed measure
before discussing it in the assembly.

if private members only =si privati tantummodo.

Both *privati* and *tantummodo*
gain stress ; for the normal order
would be *tantummodo privati.*

had risen =processissent.

For the verb cp. 30. 37. 7 cum
...Gisgo ad dissuadendam pacem
processisset.

It looks like a translation of
παρελθών used of speakers coming
forward to the βῆμα, as here to the
rostra.

to speak for or against =ad suadendum dissuadendumque.

For *que* and the verbs see on 34. 1. 4.

the measure before us

= quod ab nobis rogatur.

Cp. *legem rogare.*

I, for my part,

= ego quoque = καὶ ἐγώ.

Compare note on *tribuni quoque* above.

feeling that enough had been said on both sides

= cum satis dictum (*sc.* esse) pro utraque parte existimarem.

Here the subjunctive *existimarem* does double work, and means not merely "since I was thinking," but "since I should have been thinking (if private members only had spoken)." Such a double subjunctive is normal with the imperfect, but not with the pluperfect. Thus *ut faceret* may = "so that he would have been doing"; but "so that he would have done" requires the resolved forms *ut facturus fuerit, ut facere potuerit.* See Roby § 1521.

W. quotes 31. 38. 4 which well illustrates both constructions: *si ...copiis congressus rex fuisset,* FORSITAN *inter tumultum,* CUM *omnes* ... FUGERENT, EXUI *castris* POTUERIT *rex.* See W.'s note on the passage.

should have remained silent *and* awaited

= tacitus (ἄν)...exspectassem.

the verdict of your votes

= suffragia vestra.

The words "the verdict of" are merely ornamental and add nothing to the sense.

§ 2.　But

= nunc = νῦν δέ. See on 34. 2. 2.

a gentleman of such authority   = vir gravissimus.

Latin loves superlatives of exaggeration.

The word *vir* (contrast *homo*) implies respect and also prominence in public life.

and a consul—I mean M. Porcius   = consul M. Porcius.

There is, I think, a crescendo. The critic, says Valerius, is a public man (*vir*) of weight (*gravissimus*), our highest official (*consul*) and, above all, M. Porcius Cato.

We have a similar effect (but an anti-climax) in Cic. *Pro Caec.* 9. 28 decimo loco testis exspectatus et ad extremum reservatus dixit, senator populi Romani, splendor ordinis, decus atque ornamentum iudiciorum, exemplar antiquae religionis, Fidiculanius Falcula.

has not only used...his influence, ...but has also delivered a...oration against our proposal   = non auctoritate solum..., sed oratione etiam...insectatus sit rogationem nostram.

Here "not only" properly refers to "influence," just as "but also" properly refers to "oration." Latin and Greek are more careful than English in such matters. Moreover the two ideas "influence" and "speech" are emphasized by the order; both lie *between* the adverbial phrases *non ...solum* and *sed...etiam*.

For English carelessness in regard to the position of the negative, compare "I have not come to see him" with *non ut viderem eum veni* and οὐχ ἵνα ἴδοιμι αὐτόν, ἦλθον. So "It was not said to deaf ears"=haud surdis auribus dicta (3. 70. 7). See 34. 5. 12 on "in a case which especially touches."

used his influence...delivered a speech against
=auctoritate...oratione...insectatus sit.

English varies the expression: Latin has parallelism—two ablatives of the means and *one* common verb.

The verb gains a certain stress by preceding *rogationem nostram* —he has used his influence to *attack*, not to defend.

(influence) which needed no words to enhance it
=quae tacita satis momenti habuisset.

Lit. "which in silence (without words) would have had enough weight."

Here *tacita* (οὖσα)=*si tacita fuisset*. The metaphor in *momenti* is from a balance; Cato's *weighty* influence (*auctoritas = gravitas*) would have made the scale-pan *move* down (*momentum = movimentum*). Thus *momentum* helps to translate "the *weight* of his influence."

W. well quotes Cic. *Sull.* 82 quorum tacita gravitas loquitur.

Observe how *tacita* occurs here, despite the nearness of *tacitus* at the end of § 1.

carefully prepared
=accurata.

The comparative in this sense is more common. Compare *accuratior oratio* (35. 31. 4); *accuratior sermo* (26. 50. 3); *accuratius agere* (42. 45. 2).

Other phrases are *praeparata oratio* (35. 16. 2); and *oratio ad tempus parata* (28. 43. 1).

I am compelled to make a brief reply
= necesse est paucis respondere.

Here *paucis* = *paucis verbis* = "by means of a few words."

Note the constructions of *necesse*, e.g. "I must go" = (1) necesse est me ire; (2) necesse est mihi ire; (3) eam necesse est. In the last, the order is invariable (i.e. the subjunctive always precedes). Very rarely do we find *necesse est ut.*

§ 3. The consul, however,
= qui tamen.

When *qui* is a mere connective = *et is, sed is,* the only conjunction added is *tamen.* Obviously if *qui* = *sed is, is autem, is vero,* then *qui autem, qui vero* would be as needless as "but however." See M. § 448 Obs.

expended
= consumpsit.

The Latin has a touch of "wasted."

more verbiage
= plura verba.

on reproof of married women
= in castigandis matronis.

The noun of English ("reproof") becomes the verb of Latin.

Note how Latin uses stronger words. We say "reproof": Latin says *castigare*; we say "dislike":

Latin says *odium*; we say "criticism": Latin says *convicium*.

Observe that *in castigando matronas* would not be possible; the ablative of the gerund, *if governed by a preposition*, can only take the accusative of a neuter pronoun. Thus *in haec agendo* (in the case of doing this) is possible; but if we use *res*, we must write *in his rebus agendis*.

on criticism of our bill

= in rogatione nostra dissuadenda.

Again the noun ("criticism") becomes the verb of Latin.

For *dissuadere* see on 34. 1. 4.

Note the chiastic order *in castigandis matronis...in rogatione ...dissuadenda*. This draws attention to the double antithesis—reproof)(criticism : women)(the bill.

and he actually raised the question

= et quidem ut in dubio poneret.

Here *et quidem = et ita quidem verba consumpsit ut....*

The combination *et quidem =* "and indeed" is very common at all periods of Latin literature. As a connective it often = καὶ δή καί = "and what is more," "and further."

It may also = *idque, et id*, καὶ ταῦτα, "and that too," as in § 8 below.

raised the question

= in dubio poneret.

Lit. "placed in the (category of the) doubtful." For the neuter adjective as noun cp. 34. 2. 10 on in publico, and in this chapter § 5 in publico, and § 7 in publicum.

the course which he blamed

=id, quod reprehenderet.

Again the specific noun "course" becomes the indefinite neuter pronoun of Latin. The subjunctive responderet is sub-oblique and represents the recta id quod reprehendo.

had been adopted by these ladies

=matronae...fecissent.

The English order may be retained by making "had been adopted" active voice.

"These ladies" is a mere ornate alias for the married women already mentioned in this section. Latin boldly repeats; English varies.

of their own accord

=sua sponte.

In this phrase sua prepositive is normal.

at our instigation

=nobis auctoribus.

The English abstract > Latin concrete, "we being instigators."

§ 4. But it is the measure that

=rem—see Index.

Note no connective: adversative asyndeton.

not

=non.

For non = "and not," "but not," like the οὐ, οὐχί of Greek orators, see M. § 458, Obs. 1 ad fin.

against whom the consul levelled this—allegation

=in quos iecit...hoc consul verbo tenus.

An allegation is a verbal statement not necessarily supported by facts.

The dash before "allegation" indicates a pause, and this pause is represented by the stress on *verbo tenus* (= λόγου γε ἕνεκα, "as far as words went"); for the adverbial phrase would normally precede *iecit*; its abnormal position prepares us for the antithesis *re*. In Greek we should have λόγῳ μὲν ἐπετίμησε ταῦτα, ἔργῳ δὲ οὐδὲν παρεῖχε τεκμήριον.

For *iacere aliquid* = "level a charge," cp. 6. 14. 11. "Without discriminating between truth and falsity in his charges, he alleged that treasure in the shape of Gallic gold was being hoarded by the senators" = omisso discrimine vera an falsa iaceret, thensauros Gallici auri occultari a patribus iecit.

levelled ... though without any evidence to support his charge = iecit magis...quam ut re insimularet.

Lit. "levelled rather...than so that by means of fact he made a charge."

In full we should have *iecit magis hoc...verbo tenus quam ita iecit ut re insimularet.*

This limiting *ut* will often translate "without" + the gerund in English, e.g. "He did it without Caesar's perceiving him" = ita id egit ut Caesar non videret.

Note *re* despite *rem* at the beginning of the sentence; and observe the anticipatory position of *magis*.

§ 5. He talked of

=appellavit.

Here "He talked of" *means* "He used such and such names."

conspiracy

=coetum.

Note that there is no connective and observe coetum *et* seditionem *et*...secessionem and contrast the one "and" of English.

on the part of the women

=muliebrem.

A Latin adjective often equals a genitive of English. Compare Cic. *Att.* 14. 21. 3. "It was *done* with the courage of a man, but the thoughtlessness of a child" =acta illa res est animo virili, consilio puerili.

because our wives publicly asked

=quod matronae in publico... rogassent.

Note the repeated *matronae* ("our wives") after *matronae* ("these ladies") and *matronis* ("married women") in § 3. Contrast the variety of English.

The adverb "publicly" has stress by separation from *rogassent*; the women might have solicited their husbands in private, but not in public. For the phrase cp. *in dubio* § 3, and note at 34. 2. 10 on *in publico*.

The subjunctive *rogassent* is that of "reported reason"="because, as he said." The action of asking is antecedent to the time of *appellavit*; hence the pluperfect.

that a law...should be repealed by you

=ut legem...abrogaretis.

The English order may be retained by using the active voice

in Latin; but "now that peace... flourishing" must come before the verb; for, otherwise, the sentence, being grammatically complete at "should be repealed by you," would, in Latin, cease at "abrogaretis," and *in pace...republica* would come as a surprise.

a law whose passage was aimed against them

= legem in se latam.

The noun " passage " > the verb *latam.*

in time of war and during a period of distress

= per bellum, temporibus duris.

These are further complements to *latam*, and, properly, would lie between *legem* and *latam*; but they acquire emphasis by their position — a position which enables them to be brought close to the antithetical *in pace*. See, however, the note on 34. l. 3 (p. 32).

The whole argument is: the law was passed *not* in time of peace, *not* in time of prosperity, but in war and a period of distress.

in time of war

= per bellum.

Livy often has *per* = παρά as in παρὰ τὸν πόλεμον ("in the course of the war"). So the frequent *per eos dies* = "about that time."

and during a period of distress

= temporibus duris.

Note the asyndeton. The plural *tempora* often = "a critical period." The ablative is one of attendant circumstances.

now that peace reigns

=in pace.

Note *in* to express attendant circumstances, cp. *in re trepida.*

Observe the Livian variety *per bellum, temporibus duris, in pace.*

The metaphor of "reigns" is quite dead and needs no representation. Thus "silence reigned in the camp"=silentium in castris *fuit.*

and the state is prosperous and flourishing

=et florenti ac beata re publica.

Note this *ac* used for variety with *et* where the connected member is subdivided. Compare Cic. *Off.* 3. 1 magnifica vox et magno viro *ac* sapiente digna (M. § 433 *ad fin.*).

W. thinks *florenti* merely careless for *florente*, but it may be adjectival with *in* supplied.

[In the Ciceronian passage quoted above *sapiente* is a noun (=philosopher), not an adjective; otherwise we should have *sapienti.*]

§ 6. These and other flights of rhetoric I know there are

=verba magna...et haec et alia esse scio.

Note the absence of connective.

The phrase *verba magna=big* words, "highfalutin." The adjective of quantity, normally prepositive, comes after its noun here and therefore gains stress.

Observe *verba* here, *verbo* in § 4, and *verba* in § 3.

When verbs which take the

accusative and infinitive come last, they are slightly emphasised. So here *scio*, and below *scimus omnes*.

Note the formal *et...et*. Modern English avoids "both...and."

to be pressed into the service of exaggeration

=quae rei augendae causa conquirantur.

Lit. "which are to be (can be) sought out and got together (*con-*) for the sake of exaggeration." The *quae=ut ea=* "so as to be," "so that they are to be."

The noun "exaggeration" is expressed *verbally = res augenda*. Note *res* despite *re* and *rem* in § 4.

The quasi-preposition *causa*, like all dissyllabic prepositions, may follow its case.

we are all aware

=scimus omnes.

The adjective *omnes* has stress coming last: "we know—all of us."

Note the variety of English: "we are aware" and above "I know")(repetition of Latin: *scimus* and *scio*.

as a speaker is not merely weighty, but, sometimes, aggressive too

=oratorem non solum gravem sed interdum etiam trucem.

The effect of placing *interdum* between *sed* and *etiam* is to draw our attention to a polite qualification of *trucem*.

despite his gentle character

=cum ingenio sit mitis.

Both *ingenio* and *mitis* gain stress, the former by separation, the latter by coming last. By *nature*, says the speaker, Cato is *gentle*, but, on a platform, he may be the reverse. The whole phrase *cum...mitis* comes as a courteous and emphatic addendum, since the sentence is constructionally complete at *scimus omnes*.

§ 7. For what startling novelty

=nam quid tandem novi.

The *tandem* goes with *quid* and = "(what) pray?" = τί ποτε; translating "startling." For *novus* see note on 34. 3. 3.

these ladies

=matronae.

"these ladies"—an ornate alias for "the married women." Latin therefore puts *matronae* again, in spite of *matronae* § 5, and *matronae*, *matronis* § 3. See § 9 below.

by crowding the streets and courting publicity

=quod frequentes...in publicum processerunt ?

The metaphor "courting" is dead. All that it *means* is "have come into publicity"; this Latin writes.

The words "the streets" and "publicity" are sufficiently turned by *in publicum*.

in a matter which touches them so nearly

=in causa ad se pertinente.

Seeing that *pertinens* is here adjectival, we should expect *pertinenti*, cp. § 12. In this place "them" refers to the subject of the sentence in which it stands; therefore we have *se*)(§ 12 *ad ipsas*.

Is this the first occasion on which... ?

=numquam ante hoc tempus... ?

before the public gaze	=in publico.

Note the repetition: *in publicum* ("courting publicity") above, and in § 5 *in publico* ("publicly"). Contrast the variety of English. In § 9 below, *in publicum* = "into the treasury."

See note at 34. 2. 10 on *in publico*.

Nay, I will open your own "Antiquities," and refute you from it	=tuas adversus te Origines revolvam.

Observe the absence of connective. Note the stress on *tuas*, prepositive and separated from its noun. It emphasises the antithesis "your own against yourself," i.e. your own mouth shall convict you; you shall be hoist with your own petard.

The reference to the "Antiquities" is an anachronism. Cato did not write the work (so say Quintilian and Nepos) until he was an old man.

"To *open* a book" is *evolvere, revolvere, replicare*, since the Romans used rolls (*volumina*). "To close a book" is *de manibus ponere*.

§ 8. Hear	=accipe.

Again there is no connective. This use of *accipere* for *audire* is archaic and colloquial. See L. & S. Lucretius (e.g. 4. 983) has the full phrase *auribus accipere*.

and always	=et quidem semper=idque semper=καὶ ταῦτα ἀεί. See § 3 above.
to the interests of the state	=bono publico.

This may be a modal ablative or, as Roby § 1243 holds, an ablative of attendant circumstances. The noun is *bono*. We also get *malo publico*, and *pessimo* (= "great detriment") *publico*. Tac. *Ann.* 3. 70 has *egregium* (= honour) *publicum*. See W. on 2. 1. 3.

To begin at the beginning

=iam a principio.

Livy begins his first chapter of Book i with *iam primum omnium*. Compare 1. 2. 3 *iam inde ab initio*.

in the reign of Romulus

=regnante Rōmulo.

The noun of English > the verb of Latin.

Note the quantity of *Rōmulus* and contrast *Rĕmus*.

when the Sabines had seized the Capitol and a...battle was being fought

=cum Capitolio ab Sabinis capto ...dimicaretur.

Latin subordinates "had seized" and uses *dimicaretur* impersonally.

(when)...a pitched battle was being fought

=(cum)...signis collatis dimicaretur.

The noun "battle">the verb, and the adjective "pitched"> the adverb or, as here, the adverbial phrase *signis collatis*.

in the very midst of the forum

=medio in foro.

Note the abnormal position of *medio*. This position translates "the very" of English. Compare 7. 19. 3 *medio in foro*, and 44. 35. 16 *medio in alveo*. W. says *in medio foro* is the usual order; indeed the adjective of locality most often comes first as in *in summo monte*, etc. But at 44. 44. 4 we have *in foro medio*.

The preposition is more often omitted with the adjectives *totus, omnis, cunctus, medius.*

did not the matrons rush between ...and stay the fury of the fight?

=nonne intercursu matronarum ...proelium sedatum est?

Like ἄρα, *nonne* is frequently inserted *after* the completion of the subordinate clause, as here after *cum...dimicaretur.*

rush between

=intercursu.

The verb of English here>the noun of Latin. The converse, as we have seen, is far more common.

Note how the English order of narration may be kept by making the "matrons' rush" the means, and by using the passive verb. In fact *intercursu matronarum* is really subject, i.e. the intervention of the women stayed the fight. Thus *proelium* though grammatical subject takes a humble place in the sentence. Compare *Pref.* § 9. "The qualities which won the Empire" = quibus artibus... partum...imperium sit; 3. 62. 2. " The tactics of my colleague and the bravery of the soldiers won the day " = consilio collegae, virtute militum victoria parta est. And see 34. 6. 9 on *ne abrogata ea effundantur ad voluptatem.*

rush between the two lines

=intercursu...inter acies duas.

The prepositional phrase *inter acies* qualifying *intercursu* is doubly justified because *inter-cursu* is (1) a noun of strong verbal nature, (2) accompanied by an attribute *matronarum*. See 34. 1. 5 on *aditus in forum.*

The order *inter acies duas* is noticeable. Livy is in such haste to write how women ran between battle-lines that *duas*, though an adjective of number, is made post-positive.

stay the fury of the fight

=proelium sedatum est.

The metaphor *sedare*, properly to cause to sit, to allay, e.g. *sedare fluctus*, is frequent with *pugnam, proelium, bellum*, etc.

§ 9.   Again

=quid ?=τί δέ;=καὶ μήν.

after the expulsion of the kings

=regibus exactis.

The noun "expulsion" becomes the verb. The word *regibus* comes first like *regnante* in § 8 to remind us that we are still dealing with the early times of the *kingship.*

when Marcius Coriolanus, at the head of the Volscian legions, had encamped

= cum Coriolano Marcio duce legiones Volscorum castra...posuissent.

The important person is the general; he therefore comes first in Latin as if subject.

Note the order *Coriolano Marcio* for *Marcio Coriolano*. This inversion (rare in Cicero) is fairly frequent in Livy, and very frequent in Tacitus. When it is used in Cicero or Livy, the *praenomen* is never inserted.

had encamped within five miles	=castra ad quintum lapidem posuissent.
was it not *they* who	=nonne...matronae.

The stress on "they" is represented by the rhetorical repetition of *matronae* here and in the next sentence.

For the position of *nonne* cp. § 8 above.

the army	=id agmen.

The English definite article may often be represented by *is* or *ille*. The order is as if *id agmen* were going to be the subject.

which, otherwise, would have overwhelmed this city	=quo obruta haec urbs esset.

The relative is here logical subject and, therefore, the grammatical subject is thrust to the end. See note at 34. 5. 8 on *intercursu* and the citation from *Pref.* § 9.

The word "overwhelmed" should be read with an upward intonation; hence *obruta* comes early.

The protasis *nisi matronae avertissent* is implied, and its implication (natural to Latin) sufficiently represents "otherwise."

Furthermore	=iam = καὶ μήν.
when it had been taken by the Gauls	=urbe capta a Gallis.

Latin repeats *urbs*)(the "it" of English.

The normal order would be *urbe a Gallis capta*, but "taken" is the important point)("nearly overwhelmed" above; and *a*

Gallis comes as an after-thought and has the effect of "this time by the Gauls")(*ab Sabinis* of § 8.   Compare 35. 35. 1 quem spoliatum maritimis oppidis a Romanis)(ab Achaeis.

was not its ransom the gold (which *they* contributed to the treasury ?)

=aurum quo redempta urbs est (nonne matronae...in publicum contulerunt ?).

Again "its" is turned by the repetition of *urbs*, and again the relative is logical subject, as if "(the gold) which ransomed the city." Compare above *quo obruta ...urbs esset* and note. The stress is on "ransomed")("saved by soldiers"; hence *redempta* comes early.

The noun "ransom" > the verb. Observe that *quo...urbs est* is a mere adjectival clause, and the tense *redempta...est* is in no way affected by the tense of the principal verb *contulerunt*. Contrast the instances quoted at 34. 3. 7 on *sed tamen cum fuit*.

they

=matronae.

Again repetition in Latin. See above for this, and for *nonne* see § 8.

amid universal applause

=consensu omnium or, as at 33. 23. 1, omnium consensu.

We even get *consensu* alone, as at 3. 35. 7 and 3. 38. 7.

to the treasury

=in publicum (sc. aerarium).

§ 10. And, not to go to ancient history, in the last war

=proximo bello, ne antiqua repetam.

Observe that there is no connective. The prepositive *proximo* is contrasted with *regibus* of *regibus exactis* at the beginning of § 9.

The reference is to the Punic War.

ancient history   =antiqua.

The neuter plural translates the specific noun of English. For *repetere* compare Cic. *De Inv.* 1. 1. "When I begin to trace the events of historic narrative"=cum res... ex litterarum monumentis repetere instituo.

when there was need of money..... And also, when   =et, cum pecunia opus fuit,...et, cum.

Note the first (anticipatory) *et*, like μὲν in πρῶτον μὲν...ἔπειτα δέ.

The word *pecunia* comes first to prepare us for the antithesis *dii*, as if *pecunia μὲν...dii δέ*.

For *cum...fuit* see note on 34. 3. 7 *sed tamen cum fuit*. The second *cum* is followed by a subjunctive of attendant circumstances and the normal imperfect contemporaneous with *profectae sunt*.

did not the widows and the unmarried assist the public funds from their own?   =nonne...viduarum pecuniae adiuverunt aerarium?

The logical subject is "the widows and the unmarried"; therefore *viduarum* takes the place of the subject and is prepositive. The word *viduae* includes any husbandless woman of independent fortune.

For *nonne* cp. § 8.

Observe *pecuniae* despite *pecunia* just preceding. English varies; Latin repeats.

Note the position of *aerarium* —a single word after the verb.

when new deities were called in   =cum dii quoque novi...accerserentur.

The word "deities," if read intelligently, has stress by antithesis to *pecunia*. Livy brings this out by means of *quoque*, as if ὅτε καὶ οἱ θεοί, where καὶ = " on the other hand." Thus *novi*, though more often prepositive (cp. *novus homo*) becomes postpositive.

to aid our desperate fortunes   =ad opem ferendam dubiis rebus.

Probably *dubiis rebus* is ablative of attendant circumstances. It might be dative, but the order is against its being so.

did not our matrons, one and all   =matronae universae.

This is the eighth instance of *matronae* in this chapter)(variety of English.

The word *universae* (properly prepositive) = *cunctae*, i.e. *coniunctae* = ἅπασαι)(πᾶσαι = *omnes*. The place of the somewhat rare singular *cunctus* is supplied by *universus*.

that they might greet the Holy Mother of Ida?   =ad matrem Idaeam accipiendam?

The order of the phrase is that of a purpose clause and this may always follow the principal verb. Livy desires, also, to avoid the cacophony of *ad mare ad matrem* in juxtaposition.

§ 11. But, say you, the grounds are different

=dissimiles, inquis, causae sunt.

The stress is on "different"; hence *dissimiles* comes first. Note the absence of connective.

Well, I have not set out

=nec mihi...propositum est.

Here *nec*=ἀλλ' οὐ. Compare 1. 27. 1, and 1. 53. 1.

For *mihi*, a quasi-dative of the agent, see M. § 250 *a*.

to prove them parallel

=causas aequare.

Note the repetition of *causas* where English has a pronoun. Compare 3. 72. 6. "Greed and *its* champion won the day "= plus cupiditas et auctor cupiditatis valet, and *passim* elsewhere. See § 9 on *urbs...urbe...urbs*.

It is sufficient to make good my plea that nothing unprecedented has been done

=nihil novi factum purgare satis est.

Observe the adversative asyndeton in both languages, and note the omission of *esse* with *factum*.

For *novi*=unprecedented, see 34. 3. 3 on *novum*, and for *novum* = English noun "novelty," see 34. 2. 10 on *in publico*. The genitive *novi* is that of "the divided whole" (Roby, § 1296).

Note *purgare*+acc. and infin. ="plead by way of excuse." The verb is a favourite with Livy, who uses it (1) as here; (2) with *se* = "excuse oneself"; (3) with *crimen*, etc. = "explain away," "make excuses for"; (4) = "prove" (a rare meaning).

For (1) cp. 1. 9. 16 factum (sc. *esse*), 24. 47. 6, 28. 37. 2 ; (2) 1. 50. 8, 4. 25. 12, 6. 17. 7, 8. 32. 10, 34. 21. 2, 34. 61. 10, 35. 19. 2, 36. 32. 3, 37. 28. 1, 38. 14. 8, 42. 14. 4, 43. 4. 3, 43. 8. 1 ; (3) 8. 23. 4, 8. 37. 10, 36. 35. 11 ; (4) 9. 26. 17 *ut innocentiam suam purgarent*.

§ 12.   however

=ceterum.

The word is typical of Livy. It occurs once in Terence, once in Cicero; otherwise not before Sallust.

If...no one marvelled at what the matrons did, why...should we wonder at their action ?

=quod...fecisse eas nemo miratus est, (id)...miramur (eas) fecisse ?

Lit. " What no one wondered that they did, that thing do we wonder that they have done ? "

Observe this frequent idiom— the relative picked up by a demonstrative, either expressed or, as here, understood. [It is tempting to assume that *id* has dropped out before *in*.]

Compare "who steals my purse, (he) steals trash." So Greek ὅς ... οὗτος. Modern English prefers "He who steals...," or "He steals trash, who ...," or (as in our passage) "If anyone steals my purse, he...." We still put the relative clause first with " whoever."

Note the repetition *fecisse... fecisse*, and *miratus...est...miramur*)(the variety of English.

no one	=nemo.

Note how this is put late, because the important part of the sentence lies in the words *in rebus ad omnis* ...)(*ad ipsas.*

under conditions	=in rebus, despite *rebus* in § 10.

For *res* see Index.

Here *in* expresses attendant circumstances.

which affected everybody	=ad omnis (=omnes)...pertinentibus.
men and women alike	=pariter, viros feminas.

This in Latin goes within the phrase *rebus...pertinentibus.*

For the bi-membral asyndeton *viros feminas* see M. § 434, and compare 35. 35. 7 Antiochum... terras maria armis viris completurum.

in a case which especially touches themselves	=in causa proprie ad ipsas pertinente.

Here *ad se* would be awkward because "themselves" does not refer to the subject of the principal verb, and because *eas* (the subject of *fecisse*) is not expressed. See 34. 5. 7 on *ad se* and on *pertinente* for *pertinenti*.

The adverb "especially" really qualifies "themselves" and in Latin must come immediately in front of *ad ipsas.* English is careless in such matters. See note at 34. 5. 2 on "has not only used."

action	=fecisse.

The noun > the Latin verb.

§ 13.   Upon my soul

=me dius fidius.

This is often written *medius fidius*. Originally the phrase was *me deus fidius* (Ζεὺς πίστιος) *adiuvet*="So help me the god of pledges" (*fides, πίστις*). Compare *mehercle=me Hercules adiuvet*.

Observe that there is no connective.

our ears are the ears of tyrants

=superbas...aures habemus.

The word *superbus*=haughty, tyrannical, cp. Tarquinius Superbus.

The phrase occurs again at 24. 5. 5 only, but hardly less bold is 45. 19. 9 "his ear had already been gained" = occupatae iam aures.

Note the English method of stressing "of tyrants" = "tyrannical," and observe how Latin effects the same end by *order* i.e. *superbas* is prepositive and separated from its noun.

when masters do not disdain the prayers of their slaves

=cum domini servorum non fastidiant preces.

In English "slaves" has the upward intonation)(honourable women. Hence in Latin *servorum* is prepositive and separated from its noun. Moreover Latin is fond of grouping together antithetical terms. To a Roman *domini servorum* sounds like "To take the case of masters and slaves."

Note the position of *preces*. Livy loves a single word after the verb, especially an iambus.

we are scandalised by the entreaties

Here *cum* is followed by the subjunctive of attendant circumstances, and nearly = although.
= nos rogari...indignamur.

The noun "entreaties" > the verb *rogari*.

of honourable women

= ab honestis feminis.

The adjective is prepositive. The stress on it suggests the antithesis *improbis, impudicis (servis)*.

CHAPTER VI

§ 1.   And now I come

= venio nunc.

Again there is no connective.

to the question at issue

= ad id de quo agitur.

Here *agitur* is either impersonal or *res* may be supplied as subject.

The specific noun "question" > the Latin indefinite neuter *id*.

Here

= in quo, despite *de quo* just preceding.

the consul's speech fell under two heads

= duplex consulis oratio fuit.

The genitive *consulis* is prepositive, perhaps to draw attention to his official position.   His arguments are the arguments of a *consul*—they carry official weight, and imply official responsibility. Compare the prepositive *consularis* in § 2, and the position of *consul* at 34. 7. 14.

The word *duplex* is, of course,

predicative. Were it merely an attribute, the order *duplex consulis oratio* would be normal. See 34. 4. 12 on *aequato omnium cultu.*

first... ; secondly...   =nam et...et = τοῦτο μὲν γὰρ ... τοῦτο δέ....

Note the connective *nam.*

he strongly objected to the repeal of any law   =legem ullam abrogari est indignatus.

The noun "repeal" > the verb. The pronominal adjective *ullus* is used because "any" is emphatic, and excludes all)(*quivis, quilibet*, which include all. Thus "Anyone can jump a foot" = *quivis, quilibet*)("Can anyone jump fifty feet ?" = *num quisquam...?*

Of *quisquam* the adjective is *ullus* and from *ullus* it gets its feminine.

The rule for *quisquam* and *ullus* is: use them after negatives expressed or implied (as after a comparative); in emphatic statements (e.g. *si quisquam* = if *anyone*); to express the minimum, as in Seneca's *cuivis potest accidere quod cuiquam potest* i.e. "What can happen to *anyone* (if only one in the universe) can happen to everyone."

any whatsoever   =ullam omnino = νόμον καὶ ὁντινοῦν.

strongly objected   =est indignatus, despite *indignamur* (" we are scandalised ") at the end of the previous chapter)(variety of English.

secondly to the repeal, in particular, of a law

= et eam praecipue legem.

Note the anticipatory *eam*= " a " of English, where a relative follows. The adverb *praecipue*, which ought to precede *eam*, gains emphasis.

for the suppression of female extravagances

= quae luxuriae muliebris coercendae causa lata esset.

The noun " suppression ">the verb *coercendae*. For the gerundive to turn an abstract noun cp. 1. 1. 1 " advocates of Helen's restoration " = reddendae Helenae auctores.

§ 2. This universal defence... while the attack

= et illa (the former) communis... oratio..., et haec (the latter) adversus.

There is, I think, no connective. The first *et*=μέν or τε; the second *et*=δέ or καί.

The stiff and formal *illa...haec* —" the former "..." the latter "— while typical of Latin, is unnatural to English.

universal defence of legislation

= communis pro legibus (sc. oratio).

See note on 34. 1. 5 *aditus in forum.*

seemed a fit topic for a consul

= visa consularis oratio est.

For the prepositive (because predicative) *consularis* compare *consulis oratio* in § 1. Latin repeats *oratio*; English varies— " speech "..." topic."

Observe the separation of the auxiliary *est* from *visa*. Livy does this frequently. Perhaps here *visa* gains stress by its position. See M. § 465, Obs. 4.

the attack on luxury

=haec adversus luxuriam (sc. oratio).

See note at 34. 1. 5 on *aditus in forum*. Observe the repeated *luxuriam* despite *luxuriae muliebris* in § 1. Contrast the variety of English.

was well-suited to an austere morality

=severissimis moribus conveniebat.

The underlying idea of *severus* is fixed, rigid, puritanical. See Duff on Lucretius 5. 1190 *signa severa*, where he explains the epithet as denoting the "purity and coldness of the starlight." Probably there is an idea of fixity as well.

Thus Tennyson's "Beneath the stony face of time" would be *sub temporis ore severo*.

§ 3. there is danger that dust may be thrown in your eyes

=periculum est…ne quis error vobis offundatur.

Here *error*=liability to err, to get lost (in the darkness), and the metaphor is kept up in *offundatur* —a verb so often used with *tenebrae, nox, caligo*, etc.

The form *quis* adjectival, for *qui* is not uncommon. See M. § 90. 1.

unless we show

=nisi…docuerimus.

The verb is probably future perfect. It is future because *periculum est = aliquid mali accidet*, and future perfect because antecedent in time to *accidet*.

the fallacy which underlies each objection

=quid in utraque re vani sit.

Lit. "What of folly is in each

thing." For the neuter adjective *vani*=a noun see at 34. 2. 10 on *in publico*.

Note the separation of the genitive *vani* from *quid*. See at 34. 2. 1 on *minus...negotii*.

each =utraque—because there are *two* objections)(*quaque* of more than two.

objection =*re*.

See Index.

§§ 4, 5. Speaking for myself, I =ego enim.

The English expression is merely a way of emphasising "I")(others. Therefore *ego* is inserted. Note the connective *enim*.

Observe how in these sections we have *two* main sentences: (1) "Speaking for myself, I admit... nugatory"; (2) "On the other hand...with changing times." Contrast the *one* sentence of Latin, with its formal precision—*ego enim quem ad modum...fateor, ...sic...video*. The phrase *quem ad modum...sic = ut...ita = τοῦτο μὲν...τοῦτο δέ* = "though...yet."

The antithetical words are "I admit")("I see"; they therefore have stress, and in Latin come late; for verbs which take the accusative and infinitive come early unless emphatic.

laws which are passed...should in no case be repealed = ex iis legibus, quae...latae sunt, nullam abrogari debere.

Note the anticipatory *iis*.

are passed =latae sunt.

Here "are passed" = "have

been passed" i.e. a complete (perfect) present. Obviously the passage of a law is antecedent in time to its possible repeal. The principal verb *debere* is present; therefore the subordinate verb is present, and complete present because antecedent in time.

The indicative is not unusual in subordinate clauses of Orat. Obl. when the principal verb is 1st person. See Madv. *De Fin.* 1. 17. 55, and cp. *Pro Cluent.* 2. 6, and 57. 158.

not to meet some special need   = non in tempus aliquod.

Here, as often, *tempus* = καιρός = a critical time. The pronoun *aliquod* is abnormally postpositive, because it expresses emphatically "some special, considerable, important" occasion.

So below, *status aliquis* and *tempora aliqua*.

but (are passed) to stand for all time because of their permanent utility   = sed perpetuae utilitatis causa in aeternum latae sunt.

Observe *perpetuae* prepositive, in chiastic contrast to *aliquod* postpositive = "some special (occasion)."

Note too how "not to meet... utility" comes within the clause *quem ad modum...fateor*, whereas the limitation *nisi quam...fecit* comes, as an afterthought should do, *after* "fateor." This order is naturally common with clauses introduced by *nisi forte* and *nisi vero*.

unless either experience has proved them a mistake

= nisi quam aut usus coarguit.

Lit. (of course) "unless (it be one) which...."

Livy has at 45. 32. 7 an interesting parallel: "He gave to Macedonia laws...so wisely framed that even lengthy experience—the only true test of legislation—found nothing to which exception could be taken" = leges Macedoniae dedit...quas (= tales ut) ne usus quidem longo tempore, qui unus est legum corrector, experiendo argueret.

[In this passage note (1) how the English "nothing" comes early in Latin, so that "even... nothing" > "not even (any-thing)"; (2) the Livian pleonasm *usus...experiendo*; (3) the repetition *leges ... legum*)(English variety; (4) *longo tempore*—the ablative may be used where the adjective expresses duration. See the examples quoted by Roby § 1185, and add Caes. *B.C.* 1. 81. 3 *tota* nocte; *B.G.* 1. 26. 5 *tota* nocte *continenter* ierunt. This last justifies *B.C.* 1. 46. 1 pugnatum est *continenter* horis quinque.]

The verb *coarguere* like *arguere* in 45. 32. 7 and ἐξελέγχειν = to "show up (the weaknesses of)." Compare 34. 54. 8 veteribus, nisi quae usus evidenter arguit, stari malunt = men prefer to abide by tradition, save where experience plainly condemns.

Livy has *usus* subject to a transitive verb eleven times, but always with an inanimate object or with no object expressed. See Appendix A.

some particular condition of the body politic

=status aliquis rei publicae.

For the order of *aliquis* see above on *tempus aliquod*. The form *aliquis* for the regular adjectival *aliqui* is not infrequent.

The order of *rei publicae* seems to show that it is felt both as genitive with *status* and then again as dative (ἀπὸ κοινοῦ) with *inutilem*.

rendered nugatory

=inutilem fecit.

At 34. 27. 6 we have si quos suspectos status praesens rerum faceret.

These two are the only cases in Livy of *status* subject to a transitive verb. But *facere* with an abstract or inanimate subject is extremely common in Latin. See Appendix A.

§ 5.   On the other hand laws once demanded by special situations

=sic, answering *quem ad modum*.

=quas tempora aliqua desiderarunt leges.

For the position of *aliqua* see above, § 4 on *in tempus aliquod*.

Note the order of *leges*—a single word after the verb.

The word *tempus* occurs some 39 times in Livy as subject to a transitive verb (cp. 34. 6. 10), but in only 6 of these 39 cases is the object a person. See Appendix A.

The adverb "once" is translated by the tense of *desiderarunt* i.e. "have demanded "—complete present.

Observe that we say: "laws which special situations have demanded, I see to be...": Latin says "what laws special situations have demanded, these I see to be...." The relative is more often than not "picked up" by the demonstrative. Here we might have *eas* before *mortales*.

I see to be "mortal" (if I may use the word)

=mortales, ut ita dicam,...esse video.

The position of *video* gives it emphasis—I don't think, I know; I see the process for myself. See note at the beginning of § 4.

Livy here apologises for the bold *mortales*. At 2. 44. 8 he speaks of *imperia* (empires) as *mortalia*, without apology.

and liable to change with changing times

=et temporibus ipsis mutabiles.

The ablative *temporibus* is partly temporal, partly causal. Observe the repetition § 4 *tempus*, § 5 *tempora* and *temporibus*. Contrast the variety of English: "need," "situations," "times."

§ 6. Measures adopted in peace are generally rescinded

=quae in pace lata sunt, plerumque bellum abrogat.

Observe that there is no connective. "Measures "= *quae*, i.e. a neuter pronoun translates the specific noun of English.

Note *in pace*, where *in* expresses attendant circumstances.

generally

=plerumque.

The position of *plerumque*
(separated from *abrogat*) gives
it stress, and therefore gives it
the meaning "generally." In its
normal position (immediately
before the verb) it would probably
mean "often," for in Livy, though
not in Cicero, it usually weakens
to the sense *saepe*. So in Cicero
plerique = "most," but in Livy
usually = "many."

The word *bellum* is subject to
a transitive verb 44 times in
Livy, but *pax* only 6 times. See
Appendix A.

those adopted in war, by peace

= quae in bello, pax (sc. abrogat).

Note the asyndeton at *quae,*
almost invariable with a relative. Greek would write ἁ μὲν...ἁ
δὲ....

In directing a ship...

= ut in navis administratione.

Here *in* = "in the case of."
In the English there is a simile,
but the fact is not formally shown.
Contrast Latin which inserts "just
as" (*ut*) and ties with the preceding sentence.

some methods

= alia.

Again the Latin neuter expresses the specific noun of
English.

are of value

= usui sunt.

For the predicative dative see
Roby, *Syntax*, Pref. xxvii. sqq.

for good weather

= in secunda (sc. tempestate).

Here, again, *in* expresses attendant circumstances.

others for bad

= alia in adversa tempestate.

Both English and Latin have asyndeton here)(τὰ μὲν...τὰ δέ....

The adjectives "good" and "bad" are antithetical and therefore are stressed. Thus *secunda* is kept waiting for its noun, and *adversa* is prepositive.

§ 7. Since then these   =haec cum.

Note that *haec* precedes the conjunction of its clause, although not subject to the principal clause also. This draws our attention emphatically to *ea lex*, when we find it to be the subject of the principal sentence, and we are helped to feel that *ea lex* is a special case of a general classification *haec*.

these two types of legislation   =haec.

The loose neuter suffices. All is made plain by the preceding context. The two types are laws *in tempus aliquod* and laws *perpetuae utilitatis* (§ 4).

are inherently so different   =(cum) ita natura distincta sint
    =διάφορα πέφυκεν.

to which type, think you, does this law belong?   =ex utro tandem genere ea lex esse videtur...?

We have *ex utro* (not *ex quo*) because there are only *two* classes. For *tandem* (="pray") cp. *quis tandem? τίς ποτε;*

Note the anticipatory *ea* which allows the relative clause to follow (instead of preceding) the principal sentence.

whose repeal is proposed   =quam abrogamus.

The noun "repeal" > the verb.

The tense of *abrogamus* is "conative present" = "we are for repealing." Compare 34. 1. 7 on *quae abrogabatur.*

§ 8. Well,
is it some ancient enactment of the kings

= quid ? = τί δέ; τί γάρ;
= vetus regia lex (sc. est)... ?

The two adjectives, being emphatic, are prepositive. Note the piling up of ideas—"is it old, with an unbroken history (*vetus*), and does it date back to the kings (*rēgia*) ?"

For *vetus* see 34. 3. 3 on *novum,* and for the adjectives without connective cp. 44. 5. 3 longi duo validi asseres, and 27. 22. 12 naves longas triginta veteres.

See M. § 300, Obs. 5.

as old as the life of our city

= simul cum ipsa urbe nată.

The noun "life" > the verb in Latin.

Or

= aut.

For the use of *aut* by itself, see M. § 436.

This *aut* is frequent in enumerations. Compare the special case "two or at most three"=duo aut summum tres.

In a bi-membral question, or in any question, *aut* extends, while *an* excludes. Thus "Is he good or bad ?" = utrum bonus est an malus ? Here the answer must be "good" or "bad." Contrast estne bonus aut sapiens ? To this the answer may be "He is neither"; for the Latin sounds

to take the era following

like: "Is he good or wise or what is he?"
=quod secundum est.

Lit. "the thing which is next"
=τό γε ἐπιγιγνόμενον.

The neuter pronoun translates the specific noun "era."

when the decemvirs were appointed to draw up a code

=ab decemviris ad condenda iura creatis.

For the order see 34. 4. 12 on *aequato omnium cultu.* Here the noun *decemviris* comes first because we want the name of the new era, decemviral)(regal, to come early and ticket, as it were, the new phrase. The prepositive *regia* has already prepared us.

was it included by them in the XII Tables?

=in duodecim tabulis scripta.

Latin preserves parallelism: English has a new question formally expressed as such. Latin says: "Is it an old regal law, born with the city...or...written in the XII Tables?"

The words "by them" are not needed because they are most neatly expressed by inserting *ab* with *decemviris.*

Did our ancestors regard...and therefore must *we* fear...?

=cum maiores nostri...existimarint...nobis quoque verendum...?

For the form of sentence cp. "I am tired *and therefore* am going" = *cum fessus sim, discedo,* or, *quod fessus sum, idcirco discedo.* See 34. 6. 9 (p. 153), and 34. 7. 3 (p. 175).

Note *nobis quoque* = καὶ ἡμῖν φοβητέον.

Again English has a fresh question; Latin ties closely with the preceding by a relative, i.e. by *sine qua=ut* (so that) *sine ea*.

Observe how to translate: " I regard it (a law) as essential to the preservation of wifely honour" = sine ea non existimo decus matronale servari posse, where the noun "preservation" becomes the verb.

Did our ancestors regard it as essential to the preservation of wifely honour, and therefore must *we* fear... ?

= sine qua cum maiores nostri non existimarint decus matronale servari posse, nobis quoque verendum sit... ?

Observe that *ut sine ea* (*sine qua*) goes both with *cum...servari posse* and with *verendum sit*.

The form *existimarint* is somewhat rare in Livy, but cp. *pugnarint* 2. 46. 1.

that, in annulling it, we annul also the purity and sanctity of womanhood ?

= ne cum ea pudorem sanctitatemque feminarum abrogemus ?

The verb *abrogare* has occurred four times already in this chapter, viz. in §§ 1, 4, 6, and 7. Contrast the variety of English—"repeal," "rescind," "repeal" (noun), "annul." It occurs again in §§ 9 and 10, = "repeal" (noun), and "abolition."

§ 9.   But everyone knows

= quis igitur nescit... ?

So Greek τίς ἄρα ἀγνοεῖ τοῦθ' ὅτι...; see 34. 6. 16 on "Anyone can see."

that this is a law without precedent

= novam istam legem esse.

The point is that there has been nothing like it before; therefore *novam* comes first. For *novus* see note 34. 3. 3 on *novum*.

The law is also *recens* (i.e. has been in existence for a short time), as what follows makes clear. The speaker prefers the more invidious term *novam*, although he really means *recentem*.

The word "this" would be said with a sneer ("this precious law"); hence *istam*.

carried twenty years ago = viginti ante annis latam.

The ablative is one of "measure of difference," i.e. "before by (the measure of) twenty years."

The Lex Oppia was passed in B.C. 215 and repealed in B.C. 195, the present year.

in the consulship of Quintus Fabius and Tiberius Sempronius = Q. Fabio et Ti. Sempronio consulibus.

These words must precede *latam*, for the phrase "carried 20 years ago" is constructionally complete at *latam*, and anything that followed would gain emphasis because unexpected.

When, as here, the *praenomina* of the consuls are inserted, we more often find "bimembral asyndeton." See note 34. 1. 3.

Observe that the abstract "consulship" > concrete *consulibus*.

Without it = sine qua.

The relative acts as a connective.

women lived..., and why, pray, is there danger... ? = cum...matronae...vixerint, quod tandem...periculum est ?

The "and"="and therefore";
hence the form of expression. See
§ 8 above on "and therefore must
we fear... ?"

For this "and"="and there-
fore" cp. Perceval, *History of Italy*:
"The circuit of the walls was
immense..., *and* Frederic found
that to attack them with the
battering ram...would be in vain"
= Fredericus, cum murorum ingens
circuitus esset...sensit nequiquam
se arietes admoturum.

for all those years

= per tot annos.

Note how the phrase is brought
forward for emphasis. In *Pref.*
§ 5 we get *tot per annos* with
stress on *tot* by separation, cp.
Cic. *Cat.* 1. 7. 16 quis te...tot ex
tuis amicis...salutavit ?

lived lives beyond reproach

= optimis moribus vixerint.

Observe the stress on *optimis*
prepositive.

The ablative *moribus* is one of
attendant circumstances—"their
character (being) very good."

The tense of *vixerint* is un-
certain. It may be "historical
perfect" (see M. § 335 *a*) or "complete present." The latter is due
to the fact that *periculum est* is
present; therefore the subordinate
clause is present also, and "complete present," because antecedent
in time to *est*. This I believe to
be the true explanation of such
instances as *scio quanto in honore
apud Graecos fuerit musica*; lit.

"...how honoured it *has been*," not "was." In such a case, as in our passage, the imperfect would, of course, be impossible. (See M. § 382, Obs. 5.)

why, pray, is there danger that...?
= quod tandem (= τίς ποτε κίνδυνος), ne...periculum est?

its repeal may lead to an outbreak of voluptuousness
= (ne) abrogata ea effundantur ad luxuriam.

The noun "repeal" > verb, and, as the verb contains the point ("repeal" has stress), it comes first. If we had *ea abrogata* the sense would be "*its* repeal."

The personification of "repeal" (acting as leader) is avoided by putting *abrogata ea* in the ablative. See note on 34. 5. 8 *nonne intercursu matronarum.*

The noun "outbreak" > verb. For the phrase cp. 44. 31. 13 ad preces lacrimasque effusus. But *in* is more frequent, cp. 36. 11. 3 *in luxuriam eff.*, 25. 20. 7 *in licentiam socordiamque eff.*, 29. 23. 4 *in Venerem* (licentiousness) *eff.*, 33. 18. 18 and 35. 5. 12 *in fugam effusi* (cp. *effusa fuga* 1. 27. 10, *effusa praedandi licentia* 22. 3. 9, and *effuse populari* 41. 10. 2), and, lastly, 42. 30. 2 *in Romanos effusi*, which seems to equal *in amorem Romanorum effusi.*

§ 10. If this measure had been one of long standing
= nam si ista lex vetus...esset.

Note the connective)(English. For *vetus*)(*antiquus* see 34. 3. 3 on *novum*. Here *vetus* is a conjecture. It seems better to read *aut vetus*. The scribe's eye caught the second *aut*, and omitted *aut vetus*. Madv. *Emend. Livian.* p. 497, § 398 suggests *aut antiqua aut.*

As to *ista* see above, § 9.

or passed in order to = aut ideo lata esset, ut....

If we are to read this *aut* without a preceding *aut*, then it = "or at any rate." See M. § 436.

Note the anticipatory *ideo.*

to limit feminine indulgence = ut finiret libidinem muliebrem.

The verb "limit" has stress and therefore comes early. The order gives the effect of "to limit indulgence and in women." See 34. 1. 6.

The noun *lex* is used by Livy as a subject to a transitive verb 29 times. See note on 34. 4. 13 and Appendix A.

there would be reason to fear = verendum foret.

Lit. "there would have been being an obligation to fear."

More often the auxiliary is indicative (here it would be *erat*) with the gerund. See Roby, § 1520.

Livy often uses *foret* as a mere equivalent of *esset*; sometimes for euphony, as here and at 1. 46. **3** *ut...ultimum...regnum esset quod scelere partum foret.*

For *foret* see M. § 377, Obs. 2.

that its abolition = ne abrogata.

The noun of English > the verb. So "from the building of the city" = *ab urbe condita.*

The use of the participle is frequent both with a personal subject, and a non-personal subject. For the former cp. 1. 34. 3 " Lucumo's pride was only increased by his *marriage* with Tanaquil " = Lucumoni ... animos auxit ducta in matrimonium Tanaquil ; for the latter cp. 1. 14. 9. " Their alarm was redoubled by a *movement* from the camp " =addunt pavorem mota e castris signa.

might prove an incitement

=incitaret.

The noun of English > the verb. English could say : " might incite it *(libidinem)*," but Latin simply supplies the object in such cases.

but the grounds of its adoption

=cur sit autem lata.

The noun " adoption " > verb. Words like " ground," " reason," " cause," etc. + a genitive may often be turned by a dependent question, e.g. " I know the reason of his absence "= *scio quare absit ille.* So Greek οἶδα δι' ὅτι ἄπεστιν οὗτος.

Observe *autem* third, and see M. § 471, Obs. 1. The effect (as M. points out) is to stress *cur.*

may be seen in the circumstances themselves

=ipsum indicabit tempus.

Greek would say αὐτὰ (= the facts themselves) δείξει.

For *tempus* subject to a transitive verb see on 34. 6. 5.

Note the single word after the verb.

§ 11.

the victor of Cannae

Tarentum, Arpi, and Capua
were already in his hands

§ 12.   Rome itself was thought
to be the objective of his army

our allies had revolted

Note no connective, and observe the asyndetic style in §§ 11,
12, 13, 14, 15, 16, and 18.
= victor ad Cannas.

A prepositional phrase here
qualifies a noun of strong verbal
meaning (see 34. 1. 5 on *aditus
in forum*): *victor* equals a perfect
participle of *vinco* = *victor factus*
= νενικηκώς, νικῶν.

Livy freely uses prepositions
with names of towns, where the
neighbourhood merely is denoted.

Thus *ad Cannas* would mean
"to" or "in the neighbourhood
of C." and *a Cannis* "from the
neighbourhood of C."

= iam Tarentum, iam Arpos, iam
Capuam habebat.

Note the rhetorical repetition
of *iam* (anaphora) and contrast
English.

= ad urbem Romam admoturus
(esse) exercitum videbatur.

Note how "*It* seemed that he
would come" = "*He* seemed, was
thought to be, about to come" =
venturus esse videbatur = Greek
ἐδόκει (he was thought) μέλλειν
ἰέναι.

The noun "objective" is turned
by a verb in Latin. For the phrase
cp. *machinam admovere* (Cic. *Pro
Cluent.* § 36), and English "bring
up the guns."

= defecerant socii.

The order is effective. Hannibal was approaching; a revolt

had occurred and among the allies.

there were no soldiers to take the place of the fallen
=non milites in supplementum ...(habebamus).

Observe the position of *non*, brought forward for emphasis in this and the two following clauses.

no seamen
= non socios navales...(habebamus).

The sailors were mainly drawn from freedmen of allies and "colonists" (*coloni maritimi*).

Livy writes both *socii navales* and *navales socii* (each ten times), but always *duumviri navales*. Here he puts *socios* first to remind us, perhaps, that the *socii* had revolted.

o man the fleet
=ad classem tuendam.

The word *tueri* also includes equipping and keeping in order. Compare τὸ ναυτικὸν θεραπεύειν (Thuc. 2. 65. 7).

no money in the treasury
=non pecuniam in aerario habebamus.

slaves were being purchased to bear arms
=servi, quibus arma darentur, ... emebantur.

Here *quibus* = *ut* (in order that) *iis*....

the price for whom was to be paid to their owners
=ita ut pretium pro iis...dominis solveretur.

Of course *pro iis* properly goes with the verb *solveretur*. The genitive *eorum* governed by *pretium* would mean much the same.

When *ita* comes close to *ut*, a limitation or condition is usually implied. Literally the phrase

runs thus: "on these terms (*ita*)
viz. that (*ut*) a price *was to be
paid*"—a sort of jussive running
into a concessive subjunctive.
Compare 1. 3. 5 *pax ita convenerat
ut fluvius...finis esset*, lit. "peace
was arranged on these terms (*ita*)
namely that (*ut*) the river *was to be*
the boundary." Greek would write
ξυνέβησαν ἐπὶ τοῖσδε· τὸν μὲν
ποταμὸν εἶναι ὅρον κ.τ.λ., where
εἶναι is a survival of the infinitive
=imperative, as in Homer.

on the conclusion of hostilities
=bello perfecto.

The noun "conclusion" > the
verb. The phrase must come
within its clause *ut...solveretur*.
(Contrast English order.) Properly it qualifies *solveretur*, and
should immediately precede the
verb. But it has stress, for,
normally, the payment would
have been made at once; and,
furthermore, the order *pro iis
dominis* would produce ambiguity.

§ 13. up to the same date of
settlement
=in eandem diem pecuniae.

For the position of *pecuniae*
see 34. 1. 3 on *in medio ardore
Punici belli* (p. 31).

Observe that *dies* in the singular is feminine when it means
(1) "time," cp. *volvenda dies*,
(2) a date (as here), (3) a day
fixed for legal proceedings, cp. *die
constituta*.

For *in diem* cp. "ready *against*
our coming," and Greek ἐς τὴν
δεκάτην ἡμέραν.

the tax-farmers = publicani.

had promised to contract for the supply of = praebenda......se conducturos (esse) professi erant.

The noun "supply">the verb *praebenda*.

Note that "They contract for the building of the house" = domum aedificandam conducunt)("They call for contracts for the building of the house" = domum aedificandam locant.

For the gerundive with these words and with *curo, do, trado* etc., see Roby, § 1401 and *Pref.* lxxvi.

corn and other necessaries of war = frumentum et cetera quae belli usus postulabant.

Livy has almost the same phrase at 26. 43. 7 *quae belli usus poscunt.* For *usus* as subject to a transitive verb see on 34. 6. 4 nisi quam (legem) usus coarguit. See also Appendix A.

slaves to act as rowers...were being provided by us = servos ad remum...dabamus.

W. takes *ad remum* with *dabamus.*

the number fixed in proportion to income = numero ex censu constituto.

For *ex* = "in accordance with" = κατά + accusative, cp. *ex sententia mea*; and for the position of *ex censu* see note on 34. 4. 12 *aequato omnium cultu.*

as well as pay = cum stipendio nostro.

One is tempted to read *nostros* in agreement with *servos.*

§ 14.   all our gold and silver = aurum et argentum omne.

Note stress on *omne*: an adjective of quantity is, usually, prepositive.

(senators had set the example) =ab senatoribus eius rei initio orto.

Lit. "the beginning of the (*eius*) thing having started with (*ab*, cp. ἄρχεσθαι ἀπό) the senators."

For the typical Livian pleonasm *initio orto* cp. *Pref.* § 12 *querelae …ab initio…ordiendae rei absint.*

we were contributing to the public service =in publicum conferebamus.

So Greek ἐς τὸ κοινὸν ἐσεφέρο-μεν.

widows, unmarried women, and wards =viduae et pupilli.

For *viduae* see on 34. 5. 10.

were taking what they possessed to the treasury =pecunias suas in aerarium defe-rebant.

The plural of *pecunia* (cp. "moneys") like the plural of *for-tuna* is frequent even when we are speaking of one person.

The *aerarium* was till B.C. 83 in the Temple of Saturn at the west end of the Forum.

The *de* of *defero* is probably due to the fact that people had to come *down* to the Forum from their residences on the hills of Rome. Compare *in forum de-scendere* and, perhaps, *ad accu-sandum descendere* (Cic. *Caec.* 1. 1) and *in causam descendere* (Cic. *Phil.* 8. 2. 4, and Livy 36. 7. 6).

it was provided by law =cautum erat.

Cicero often adds *in lege, in legibus*; Silver writers have *lege, legibus.*

that we should have at home not more than a certain amount of... gold =quo ne plus auri...domi habe-remus.

Lit. "there was laid down (the

amount) than which not more of gold...we were to have."

The *quo* is ablative of comparison, and *haberemus* is dependent jussive.

W. quotes the fuller form of expression from Suet. *Jul.* 19 *cautum est de numero gladiatorum, quo ne maiorem habere liceret=* "The law laid down the maximum number of gladiators which a man might possess." A good instance too is Cic. *ad Fam.* 7. 2. 1 *praefinisti quo ne pluris emerem=* "you fixed the price beyond which I was not to go"; lit. "you fixed the price (sc. *pretium*) than which not at more I was to buy."

of wrought gold and silver
=auri et argenti facti.

Contrast *infecti=* "unwrought," and *signati=* stamped, coined.

or
=quo ne plus.

Observe the rhetorical anaphora of Latin.

of silver and bronze coin
=signati argenti et aeris.

Note that *signati* is prepositive, thus forming a chiasmus with *argenti facti* preceding.

§ 15.   at such a time, were the wives so given up to luxurious adornment... ?
=tali tempore in luxuria et ornatu matronae occupatae erant... ?

Livy uses either *in* + ablative, or the plain ablative with *occupatus*. The latter construction is less frequent.

The word "so" is required here in English, and its omission is rare in Latin. Indeed the rule may be laid down that *ut* con-

secutive must have some anticipatory word in the principal
clause such as *adeo, ita,* etc. Perhaps *ita* has dropped out before
in, or should be read in place of
in.   Livy, however, omits *ita* at
3. 44. 1 and 9. 5. 6.

Observe the hendiadys *luxuria
et ornatu,* and compare 34. 7. 5
"bitter indignation" = dolor et
indignatio (p. 180).

Here *luxuria* and *ornatu* come
early because they are logical
subjects, as if the sentence ran:
"did luxurious adornment fill the
thoughts of the wives...?"

that the Oppian law was needed
for its repression ?

= ut ad eam coercendam Oppia
lex desiderata sit.

The noun "repression" > a
verb *coercendam.*

The repression of luxuriousness
is the important idea and therefore comes early.

In the hendiadys *luxuria et
ornatu* the first word is the more
emphatic and *eam* is made to
agree with it.

Observe *Oppia* prepositive as
at 34. 1. 2 *de Oppia lege abroganda.*   Here there is a variant
lex Oppia, and Madvig, *Emend.
Livian.* p. 497, § 398, would omit
Oppia on the ground that a
general reference to a law is
better suited to the context.

The aorist perfect (*desiderata
sit*) is frequent in Livy in a
consecutive clause (cp. 34. 14. 8

reprehenderit). Cicero, however, prefers the imperfect subjunctive; he still felt that the subjunctive should express a tendency rather than an *actual* result. Thus in " he is foolish enough to do it " (*ita stultus est ut id faciat*) we have a legitimate use of the mood = ὥστε +infinitive; but in " he is so foolish that he does it " (*ita stultus est ut id faciat*) we get an actual result expressed by the subjunctive = ὥστε + indicative. This is really an illegitimate extension of the subjunctive, and, in past time, Cicero salved his conscience, as it were, by using a tense of incompletion—the imperfect.

Why, owing to the abandonment of Ceres' sacrifice = cum, quia Cereris sacrificium... intermissum erat.

The noun " abandonment " > the verb.

The genitive *Cereris* is prepositive because *her* festival, being a woman's festival, ought not to have been abandoned by women.

(for all the women were in mourning) = lugentibus omnibus matronis.

The words *lugere* and *luctus* are properly used of mourning for the dead.

The phrase must, of course, be set within the clause *quia... intermissum erat*; otherwise it would brim over and acquire unnecessary emphasis. Note the repetition *matronis* after *matronae* above)(variety of English " women "..." wives."

the senate commanded that the period of such mourning should be limited to thirty days!

=senatus finiri luctum triginta diebus iussit.

Note the stress on *finiri* coming early, as if "ordered that there should be an *end* of mourning and within thirty days."

The ordinary period of mourning was ten months.

The ablative *triginta diebus* is ablative of "time within which." See M. § 276, Obs. 5.

At 22. 56. 5 Livy stresses *triginta* by making it postpositive. The whole passage deserves quotation—*adeoque totam urbem opplevit luctus, ut sacrum anniversarium Cereris intermissum sit* (note the aorist perfect in a consecutive clause), *quia nec lugentibus id facere est fas nec ulla in illa tempestate* (i.e. after Cannae) *matrona expers luctus fuerat. itaque ne ob eandem causam alia quoque sacra publica aut privata desererentur, senatus consulto diebus triginta luctus est finitus.*

§ 16.   Anyone can see

=cui non appāret...?

The positive assertion of English may often be translated by a negative question in Latin and Greek. Here *cui non apparet?* =πῶς οὐ δῆλον...; Compare 34. 6. 9 "But everyone knows"=quis igitur nescit... ?

that the...distress *in* the country

=miseriam civitatis.

For the genitive see 34. 1. 5 on "in the city"=*urbis* (p. 39).

when

="in that," "because"=quia.

every private citizen had to divert his money to the public use

= omnium privatorum pecuniae in usum publicum vertendae erant.

In Latin the logical subject "every private citizen," although not nominative, comes first. This prepositive genitive is answered by *publicum*—postpositive and chiastic.

For *pecuniae* see 34. 6. 14.

were responsible for this piece of legislation

= istam legem scripsisse.

The word *istam* (1) = "that to which you (Cato) refer"; (2) contains a sneer and represents "piece of" in the English.

The personification of *inopiam* and *miseriam* as drawing up a law is very bold. The nearest approach is at 9. 13. 9 *profectos...inopia vexavit*, and 40. 14. 2 *miseria haec et metus crāpulam facile excusserunt*.

Livy has *inopia* seven times subject to a transitive verb (only twice with a *personal* object), and *miseria* thrice (never with a *personal* object). See Appendix A.

which was to remain on the statute book only so long as

= tam diu mansuram, quam diu.

The phrase "on the statute book" is merely ornamental, and needs no reproduction in Latin.

Note the anticipatory *tam diu* formally picked up by *quam diu*. This anticipatory phrase helps to translate "only" of English. Compare "he only did it to pain her" = *eo* rem fecit *ut* dolore afficeret eam.

(so long as) the reason for its enactment continued to exist

= (quam diu) causa scribendae legis mansisset.

Note "reason for" > "reason of"; see 34. 1. 5 "in the city"= *urbis* (p. 39).

The noun "enactment" > verb. Observe the repetition *scripsisse... scribendae*)(variety of English "responsible for"..."enactment."

The pronoun "its" is turned by *legis* after *legem* above. Compare 3. 72. 6. "But greed and *its* champion won the day"=sed plus cupiditas et auctor cupiditatis valet.

continued to exist   =mansisset.

Again repetition—*mansuram* above)(variety of English "to remain on the statute book"..."continued to exist."

The pluperfect represents a future perfect in the recta, i.e. *inopia...legem scripsit* (has framed) *tam diu mansuram quam diu causa ...manserit*, where *tam diu mansuram=quae tam diu manebit*.

The tense *manserit* becomes *mansisset* to suit the past tense *scripsisse*.

§ 17. For if the measures   =nam si, quae.

The neuter plural translates the specific noun of English.

then decreed by the senate or passed by the assembly   =(quae) tunc...aut decrevit senatus aut populus iussit.

Note the first anticipatory *aut*. English does not need its insertion.

Observe too the elaborate chiasmus *decrevit senatus...populus iussit*.

to meet the circumstances of the moment
= temporis causa.

Note the repetition of *causa* just after *causā* at the end of the preceding section.

The two words are brought forward (of course within the relative clause) for emphasis, and prepare us for the contrast—*in perpetuum*. Again *tempus* = καιρός.

ought to hold good for all time
= in perpetuum servari oportet.

why do we refund moneys to private persons?
= cur pecunias reddimus privatis?

For *pecunias* see on 34. 6. 14. Note the repetition *privatis* after *privatorum* in § 16)(English variety: "private citizen"..."private person."

Here *privatis* is put last to contrast it with *publica* in the next sentence.

The *re* in *reddo* not merely expresses "back," but also "what is due." Compare *reddere epistulam* = to deliver a letter; Greek ἀποδιδόναι ἐπιστολήν with ἀπό as in ἀπαιτεῖν.

Why do we call for state contracts?
= cur publica...locamus?

Here, again, the neuter plural (aided by the sense of *locare*) translates the specific noun ("contracts") of the English.

For *locare* and *conducere* see on 34. 6. 13 (p. 160).

on the basis of immediate payment
= praesenti pecunia.

Lit. "at the (price of) money paid in cash (*praesenti*)."

Compare *pecuniam repraesentare* (Cic. *Att.* 12. 25. 1) and Livy 36. 4. 7 *stipendium...praesens dare*;

44. 27. 9 *talenta ... praesentia dare*; 44. 25. 12 *partem (pecuniae)...praesentem ferre* (=carry off); 45. 42. 11 *pretium eorum ...praesens exigere.*

The adjective *praesenti* is prepositive in contrast with the delayed payment of § 13.

§ 18. Why are slaves not bought to serve in our armies?

=cur servi, qui militent, non emuntur?

Here *qui*=*ut* (in order that) *ii.*

Why do we not, as individuals, provide rowers, ... ?

=cur privati non damus remiges...?

Note the repetition *privati, privatis* (§ 17), *privatorum* (§ 16), and contrast the variety of English: "as individuals"..."private persons"..."private citizen."

Observe the single word *remiges* after the verb, as so often. Here, perhaps, the position suggests the contrast *qui militent.*

exactly as

=sicut=ὥσπερ καὶ (τότε).

we provided them before

=tunc dedimus.

English could say "exactly as we *did* before." Latin, more often, uses repetition of the verb, and leaves the object *to be supplied.* The "vicarious" *facere* is, of course, found in Latin. See Holden, *De Off.* 1. 1. 4. So Greek uses ποιεῖν (Plato, *Rep.* 359 B) and δρᾶν (Thuc. 2. 49. 5).

CHAPTER VII

§ 1. All other classes, all other persons

= omnes alii ordines, omnes homines.

Note no connective.

Normal Latin would be *ceteri omnes*, but Livy uses *alii* for *ceteri* frequently.

are to feel the improvement in the condition of the state

= mutationem in meliorem statum rei publicae sentient.

Lit. "the change of the state to a better position." The word "better" is prepositive and has stress; it is a change (as Greek would say) ἐς τὸ βέλτιον καὶ οὐ τὸ χεῖρον.

The prepositional phrase *in meliorem statum* may qualify *mutationem* because *mutationem* is accompanied by an attribute *rei publicae*. See 34. 1. 5 on *aditus in forum* (p. 40).

and shall only our wives reap no benefit... ?

= ad coniuges tantum nostras... fructus non perveniet ?

Observe the stress on *ad coniuges* coming first. The "and" of English is turned by asyndeton. Greek would have μέν with "all other classes," and δέ with *ad coniuges*. These two words occupy the place of the subject, thrusting the grammatical subject *fructus* quite late in the sentence.

Cicero would use *solum* for *tantum*. With him *tantum* still means "so much" or "only so much."

benefit from its peace and tranquillity?

= pacis et tranquillitatis publicae
fructus...?

Note how "benefit from" >
"benefit of," and see note at 34.
1. 5 "in the city" = *urbis* (p. 39).

The genitives are prepositive
and form, as it were, a second
subject, as if Livy were writing:
"to our wives shall *peace and
tranquillity* bring no benefit?"

its

= publicae, despite *rei publicae*
above. Latin repeats; English
varies. See also note on *legis* in
§ 16 of the last chapter (p. 167).

§ 2. Purple will be worn by
us men

= purpura viri utemur.

Again there is no connective.
The Latin order makes *purpura*
the logical subject, and *purpura*
tickets, so to speak, the whole
paragraph; "purple" is to be the
topic.

in the official dress of magistrates
and priests

= praetextati in magistratibus, in
sacerdotiis.

Lit. "wearing the *toga praetexta* (as) in the case of magistracies
and priesthoods."

Observe the bi-membral asyndeton, especially common when
examples are cited in illustration.
See M. § 434, where Cic. *De Off.*
1. 16. 50 is quoted (in quibus
(feris) inesse fortitudinem saepe
dicimus, ut in equis, in leonibus).
The *ut* of this passage suggests
that *ut* may have fallen out between *praetextati* and *in*.

For the form *praetextatus* cp.
tŏgatus, tŭnĭcatus, săgatus, sŏ-

our children

will wear

the toga bordered with purple

magistrates in colonies and provincial towns...will receive from
us the right

and here, in Rome, the lowest
official class, the superintendents
of streets

leatus, călĭgatus, and English
"booted," "sandalled," "slippered."
= liberi nostri.

For *liberi*)(*pueri* see on 34.
4. 18 (p. 108).

= utentur, despite *utemur* above)(
the variety of vowel sound in
English "will be worn"..."will
wear."

= praetextis purpura togis.

For the order see on 34. 4. 12
aequato omnium cultu. Latin has
the plural *togis* attracted to the
number of the subject. Apart
from the evil sound and obscurity
of *praetextā purpurā togā*, the
singular *togā* might mean one
toga in which to wrap up the
whole family.

The *prae* of *praetexo* = "at the
edge," just as *praefringo* = I break
off *the end of* something. So
Verg. *Aen.* VI. 4 litora curvae —
praetexunt puppes = fringe the
shore.

= magistratibus in coloniis municipiisque...ius permittemus.

In Latin, of course, "in colonies" does not properly qualify
magistratibus but goes with the
verb *permittemus.*

For *coloniae* and *municipia* see
Ramsay's *Antiquities*, pp. 88–92
(Ramsay and Lanciani, pp. 118–
122).

= hic Romae infimo generi, magistris vicorum...(ius permittemus).

and here

=hic.

Note the asyndeton, as if *hic δέ* were preceded by *magistratibus μέν*.

official class

=generi.

The word "official" needs no representation ; it is already expressed in the preceding *magistratibus.*

the right to use this same dress

=togae praetextae habendae ius.

We say "right to use"; Latin can only say "right of using." See 34. 1. 5 "in the city"=*urbis.*

The phrase *toga praetexta* is repeated, despite *praetextis...togis* above)(variety of English.

§ 3. and not merely in life may they have this uniform

=nec (sc. permittemus) ut vivi solum habeant [tantum] insigne.

W. is astonished at the position of *solum* and Madvig brackets it. But there is no reason for surprise ; Livy wishes to emphasise *vivi* in contrast with *mortui,* which is put last, after its verb *crementur,* to reinforce the antithesis.

There are plenty of instances of one word, the word of interest, placed between *non* and *solum* (cp. 5. 42. 3 *non mentibus solum... sed,* etc.), and here the *ut* cannot well be placed elsewhere.

have

=habeant, in spite of *habendae* at end of previous section)(variety of English.

this uniform :

=[tantum] insigne.

H. J. Müller brackets *tantum.* Perhaps *tantum* should be read in place of *solum,* which may have been a gloss on *tantum* to show that *tantum* does not go with *insigne*; or, possibly, *tantum* was a gloss on *dumtaxat* below, and has been displaced.

Even if *tantum* could stand for *tam splendidum*, Valerius would be stultifying his argument; for he is trying to show that the *insigne* is commonplace and allowed to the most insignificant officials.

when dead they may be cremated with it

= sed etiam ut cum eo crementur mortui.

Note *mortui* last)(*vivi* at the beginning of the clause.

The colon after "uniform" is translated by *sed*, and the stress on "dead" is represented partly by *etiam*, partly by the position of *mortui*.

Shall we then deny the use of purple to none but women?

= feminis dumtaxat purpurae usu interdicemus?

Livy uses *dumtaxat* = "only." Compare 37. 53. 9 nec animum dumtaxat (= nec animum modo) vobis fidelem.....praestitit, sed omnibus interfuit bellis. The word originally meant "while it touches," "as far as it is concerned." Thus in Cic. *De Or.* 1. 58. 249 *ad hoc dumtaxat* = "for this at any rate." See Wilkins *ad loc.*

The case of *feminis* is dative and of *usu* ablative, cp. 5. 3. 8 interdicitis patribus (dat.) commercio (abl.) plebis = "you forbid patricians to have intercourse with the plebs." Lewis and Short wrongly quote *interdicere* with the accusative of the person at Caes. *B. G.* 6. 13. 6. There the dative has to be supplied; no actual object is expressed.

For the position of *feminis* cp. 34. 7. 1 *ad coniuges tantum.*

The genitive *purpurae* is pre-positive, because it, not *usu,* carries the point.

You, the husband, may have... and will you not allow...? = et cum tibi viro liceat...non sines?

Note the connective *et.* For the Latin form of expression, see note on 34. 6. 8 "and therefore must we fear...?" and on 34. 6. 9 "and why pray is there danger...?" (p. 153).

(may) have purple for your hangings = (liceat) purpura in vestem stragulam uti.

For *vestis stragula* see Becker, *Gallus,* p. 287. The phrase includes all ornamental coverings.

For *in vestem...uti* cp. 37. 15. 7 *in duas...res id usui fore*; 4. 6. 2 *utiliter in praesens certamen*; 5. 18. 3 *rei maxime in hoc tempus utili.*

the mistress of your household = matrem familiae tuam.

The phrase is *mater familiae* —practically a compound noun; hence *tuam* not *tuae.* Contrast the English.

The old genitive *familias* (cp. φιλίας), which is common with *pater* in other authors, is not used by Livy at all (W. on 1. 45. 4).

to wear that colour in her mantle = purpureum ămĭculum habere.

The English *means* "to have a mantle of purple," and this is what we find in the Latin. But the repetition "of purple" is wearisome in English. Latin, however, allows itself no greater variety than an adjective *purpureum*, instead of a genitive *purpurae*. The adjective is prepositive like the genitive *purpurae* above, and for the same reason.

to wear = habere, in spite of *habeant* ("may have") above, and *habendae* ("use") in § 2)(the variety of English.

Are the caparisons of your horse to be more brilliant than the dresses of your wife? = et equus tuus speciosius instratus erit quam uxor vestita?

Note the connective *et*.

The nouns "caparisons" and "dresses" > verbs. The antithesis is expressed by parallel order. Livy might have used chiasmus by writing *vestita uxor*.

For *instratus* cp. 21. 54. 5 instratisque equis signum exspectare.

Add both instances to Lewis and Short, and others quoted by W. at 21. 27. 9.

§ 4.   which wears out and is wasted = quae teritur absumitur.

For the bi-membral asyndeton see 34. 3. 4 and M. § 434.

I can see some reason, however unjust, for parsimony. = iniustam quidem, sed aliquam tamen causam tenacitatis video.

For the form of expression and the different idiom of English cp. 2. 24. 4.   "But their deliberations concerning a part of the state, however great that part might be, had been interrupted by fears for the country as a whole "=ceterum deliberationi de maxima quidem illa, sed tamen parte civitatis metum pro re publica intervenisse.

With *sed tamen* the word of antithetical interest (as *aliquam* here) often comes between the *sed* and the *tamen*.

Livy is the first to use *quidem* freely, attached directly *to all parts of speech*, as an exact equivalent of μέν, and followed by *sed, autem, vero*, etc. = δέ. Here *quidem* is attached to an adjective. For other parts of speech cp. 1. 50. 3 (with adverb); 34. 11. 3 (with verb); 35. 34. 2, 36. 23. 1 (with noun); 33. 39. 7 (with pronoun).

For Cicero's limitation in the use of *quidem* see M. § 489 *b*.

reason *for* parsimony   = causam tenacitatis.

For the genitive see 34. 1. 5 on " in the city "=*urbis* (p. 39).

The word *tenacitas* is rare and of this metaphorical sense (=*parsimonia*) no other example is quoted. The adjective *tenax* (= " frugal," " parsimonious ") is not uncommon ; cp. Cic. *Cael.* 15. 36 patre parco ac tenaci.

The important word is " reason " and therefore *tenacitatis* is left postpositive, although the normal order would be *aliquam tamen tenacitatis causam*. See on 34. 4. 12 *aequato omnium cultu*.

I can see = video.

The "can" of English is idiomatic but quite unnecessary.

But in the matter of gold, = in auro vero.

Note *vero* (= but) after *sed* preceding ; so μέντοι is used after a preceding δέ.

where = in quo.

Note the repetition of *in* + ablative = "in the case of," viz. *in purpura...in auro...in quo* and contrast the variety of English "in the case of,"..."in the matter of"..."where."

if we except the cost of workmanship = praeter manupretium.

there is no loss in value = nihil intertrimenti fit.

At 32. 2. 2 we have *intertrimentum argenti* = "loss through melting off." Compare *detrimentum*. Both words are from √terere (τρίβειν).

why should we be grudging ? = quae malignitas est ?

Apparently this = quae ratio malignitatis est ?

Perhaps we ought to read : *quae malignitatis est?* and supply *causa* with *quae* out of *causam* above.

Rather it is a safe investment = praesidium potius in eo est.

Observe the adversative asyndeton = "*Nay*, a security, not a loss, is entailed." Hence *praesidium* precedes *potius* and has stress.

The Greek for *in eo est* is ἐν
αὐτῷ ὑπάρχει, cp. τὰ ὑπάρχοντα
="investments," "capital."

for private and public needs

=et ad privatos et ad publicos
usus.

Note the anticipatory *et* before
ad privatos, and observe that both
adjectives are prepositive because
antithetical.

as, in fact, you have found out by
experience

=sicut experti estis=ὥσπερ καὶ
πεπειραμένοι ἴστε.

For *sicut* cp. 34. 6. 18, and for
the facts see 34. 5. 9.

§ 5. It was urged that no
rivalry exists

=nullam aemulationem.....esse
aiebat.

The verb of saying, coming
late, gains stress=he *said* so, but
it is not true.

The absence of a subject to
aiebat is remarkable, but compare
inquit at 34. 3. 9. Has *is* dropped
out after *estis* at the end of § 4?

rivalry...between individual women

=aemulationem inter se singularum.

The preposition "between" is
translated by the genitive. See
34. 1. 5 on "in the city"=*urbis*.

The use of *se* in *inter se* is
justified by the fact that *singularum* is a *subjective* genitive, as
if Livy had written: *non aemu-
lari inter se singulas*.

now that none of them possesses
gold

=quoniam nulla haberet.

Here *quoniam* retains much of
its original sense *quom iam*, where
quom (*cum*) approaches the causal
meaning, cp. *cum* in the next
sentence.

For *nulla* as a feminine of *nemo* cp. 34. 4. 6 (p. 91).

With *haberet* the object *aurum* is easily supplied in Latin. The recta is, of course, *quoniam nulla habet.* The mood of *haberet* is due to Orat. Obl., and the tense to the time of *aiebat.*

But, surely,   =at hercule.

For *hercule* see 34. 5. 13 on *me dius fidius.*

our women as a class feel the bitterest indignation   =universis dolor et indignatio est.

The word *universis* (contrast *singularum*) is logical subject and therefore comes first.

For the hendiadys cp. 34. 6. 15 " luxurious adornment "=in luxuria et ornatu (p. 163).

Remember that *universus* provides a singular to *cuncti* (*cunctus* is rare), and in the plural, as here, =" all taken together " (ἀπάσαις contrasted with καθ' ἑκάστην).

when they see   =cum...vident.

For *cum* = " because," " in that," see 34. 4. 13 *ad fin.*, and W. on 8. 33. 10.

they see the wives of Latin allies permitted such ornaments   =sociorum Latini nominis uxoribus vident ea concessa ornamenta.

The genitives *sociorum Latini nominis* are prepositive because the implied antithesis is that *Roman* wives cannot do these things (whatever Latin allies may do).

Note the double genitive. The construction is inoffensive because *socius Latini nominis* is practically one word.

In such phrases *nomen=gens* ="tribe," "nation."

The *socii Latini nominis* were those who joined in the original confederation with Rome.

The words *sociorum Latini nominis uxoribus* come early in antithesis to *sibi* below. The verb *vident* here = ἐφορῶσι = "live to see," "see with their own eyes," cp. *Pref.* § 5, 1. 46. 8, 6. 34. 10, 21. 53. 5, etc.

permitted such ornaments   =ea concessa ornamenta.

Note the anticipatory *ea=talia* preparing us for the relative clause. Observe *concessa* prepositive)(*adempta*. Greek would write δεδομένα καὶ οὐκ ἀπεστερημένα.

as are denied to themselves   =quae sibi adempta sint.

Lit. "which have been taken from them." The *sibi* is normal, standing in a subordinate clause of Or. Obl., and referring to the principal subject. The dative is that of disadvantage.

§ 6.   when they see them conspicuous in gold and purple   =cum insignis eas esse auro et purpura.

The verb (*vident*) is readily supplied in Latin.

Observe the stress on *insignis* (=*insignes*) preceding *eas.*

The ablatives *auro et purpura* are causal.

and driving through the city, while they themselves follow on foot
= cum illas vehi per urbem, se pedibus sequi.

Note the rhetorical anaphora *cum* (*vident*), and contrast the "and" of English.

The verb *vehi* is brought forward in antithesis to *pedibus sequi*. There is a certain stress, too, on *per urbem*, i.e. wives of allies drive through the Roman capital in which Roman wives must walk.

Note *illas*, referring to the same persons as *eas* above. The pronoun *ille* is frequent in contrasts (cp. *hic...ille* = "the latter" ..."the former") and this may account for the change of pronoun.

In poetry we find *hic* and *ille* referring to the same person, cp. Verg. *Geor.* IV. 396–8, Martial 3. 5. 5. In Greek οὗτος and ὅδε are used of the same person, cp. Eur. *Med.* 1046, Soph. *Ant.* 296, 750–1, and *passim* in tragedy. Thucydides has different pronouns for the same person at 4. 73. 4 and 6. 61. 7.

while they themselves
= se.

Note the adversative asyndeton = αὐταὶ δὲ after ἐκείνας μὲν (*illas*).

on foot
= pedibus.

An instrumental ablative.

as if the administration were centred not in their own community, but in the communities from which those others come
= tamquam in illarum civitatibus, non in sua imperium sit.

Latin loves parallelism; it has expressed the antithesis in the·

order *illas...se*, and therefore continues in that order, i.e. "as if in the communities of those women and not in their own (community) the imperium was."

For "and not"=*non* see M. § 458, Obs. 1 *ad fin.* So in the Greek orators οὐ, οὐχὶ and μή ="and not," "but not."

as if...were

=tamquam...sit.

The subjunctive is that of non-fact (compare with *non quod*).

The tense in such clauses of comparison is determined by the tense of the principal verb. Here *vident* is present ; therefore *sit* is present also.

The phrase "were centred in" is mere ornament for "were in "; hence *in sua...sit.*

Observe how late the *grammatical* subject (*imperium*) comes. Livy's order sounds as if *in illarum civitatibus* were subject, i.e. "as if the communities of those women, and not their own community, *contained the seat of government.*"

The words "from which those others come " *mean* nothing more than "of those others." Therefore write *illarum.* The genitive is prepositive to prepare us for the antithesis *sua,* with which *civitate* is readily supplied.

§ 7. Such a contrast could wound the feelings of men

=virorum hoc animos vulnerare posset.

Note no connective.

The antithesis is men)(women; therefore *virorum* is prepositive, separated from its noun, and placed first in the sentence.

such a contrast   =hoc.

The neuter pronoun expresses the specific noun of English.

The non-personal subject (*hoc*) with a *non-personal object* of a transitive verb is frequent enough. Livy so uses *hoc, haec* twenty-three times, and in eight of the instances the object is *animum, -os.* A *personal* object is found in five cases, and in four of them the verb is *movere.* See Appendix A.

could wound   =vulnerare posset.

Lit. "could have been wounding." The same meaning can be given by the indicative of the auxiliary, e.g. *vulnerare poterat*)(*vulnerare potuit*="could have wounded."

how much more of weak women... ?   =quid muliercularum censetis... ?

The full expression would be: " quid muliercularum animos censetis hoc vulnerare posse ?" =" what a wound (*quid* is internal accusative with *vulnerare*) do you think that this could make in the minds of weak women ?"

Note the contemptuous use of the diminutive. Diminutives have two uses, (1) affectionate, (2) contemptuous (as here). Thus *servulus* may=(1) a favourite slave, (2) a miserable, despicable slave.

who are affected by the merest trifles

=quas etiam parva movent.

Livy has a similar ungallant remark at 6. 34. 7, ceterum is risus stimulos parvis mobili rebus animo muliebri subdidit = "the laugh acted like a goad on a woman's mind affected by the merest trifles."

the merest trifles

=etiam parva.

The neuter of Latin translates the specific noun of English.

Note *parva* subject to a transitive verb with a personal object. Livy uses *movere* with a non-personal subject and a personal object without any hesitation.

§ 8.

Note (1) no connective; (2) how the negative comes early in Latin)(English ; (3) the series—*non... nec...nec...nec...nec* = οὐ...οὐδὲ... οὐδὲ...οὐδὲ...οὐδὲ; (4) *nec dona aut spolia*, where *aut*, like *ve*, connects two closely bound members of negative groups; cp. note on 34. 1. 3, neu iuncto vehiculo in urbe oppidove... ; (5) *contingere*, as so often, used of pleasant things)(*accidere* of what is unpleasant; (6) the hexameter ending—contingere possunt. Livy is not seldom guilty of this.

§ 9.

Note the adversative asyndeton.

It seems impossible to draw a clear distinction between the first three words. A ribbon in the hair would come under *munditiae* ; necklets, brooches, bracelets under *ornatus*; and *cultus* is, perhaps, dress in general.

Note how Latin inserts all the connectives (here *et...et*), or omits all, or puts *que* with the last member.

Observe *haec*—the neuter referring to a series of things which vary in gender. See M. § 214 *b*.

The genitive *feminarum* is prepositive)(*virorum*.

these are their delight and pride

= his gaudent et gloriantur.

The nouns, as so often, become verbs in Latin. The ablative *his* is causal.

these are what our forefathers called "the adornment of woman"

= hunc mundum muliebrem appellarunt maiores nostri.

Note the attraction of "these" to the number and gender of *mundum*. Compare Vergil's *hoc opus, hic labor est*.

Here, as in 32. 40. 11 non aurum modo iis, sed postremo vestem quoque mundumque omnem muliebrem ademit, the phrase *mundus muliebris* is general in meaning. The jurists restricted it to mirrors, unguents, vases, manicuring apparatus.

Note *haec...his...hunc*—anaphora with change of case, called πολύπτωτον. See Cic. *Pro Cluentio*, 14. 41, and Fausset's note *ad loc*.

The words *maiores nostri* come last, with a certain stress which playfully hoists old-fashioned Cato with his own petard.

§ 10. In mourning, what do they do but lay aside their gold as well as their purple?

=quid aliud in luctu quam purpuram atque aurum deponunt?

Note no connective.

With *quid aliud* supply, as so often, *faciunt*. See on 34. 2. 12.

Observe *in* with *luctu* (=*cum lugent*) expressing attendant circumstances.

Here *atque* is in its original sense, viz. *ad*+*que*="and in addition," "and what is more." Hence the order of the English is inverted in the Latin.

When mourning is over, what do they do but resume them?

=quid, cum eluxerunt, sumunt?

In full this would be *quid aliud faciunt, cum eluxerunt, quam sumunt (purpuram atque aurum)?*

The mood of *eluxerunt* is frequentative indicative. The tense is complete present; present because *faciunt* and *sumunt* are present, and complete present because antecedent in time to the time of *faciunt* and *sumunt*.

The *e* of *eluxerunt* expresses completion, cp. the *ex* of *exaedificare*.

If they give thanks or offer supplications, what...?

=quid in gratulationibus supplicationibusque...?

The *in* expresses attendant circumstances (cp. *in luctu* above) or ="in the case of."

Note the rhetorical anaphora and asyndeton *quid aliud...quid ...quid...?*

do they add save greater splendour in apparel?

= nisi excellentiorem ornatum adiciunt?

The adjective *excellentiorem* is prepositive because splendour, not apparel, is the point.

§ 11. Of course

=scilicet.

The whole paragraph is bitterly ironical.

if you repeal the Oppian law

=si legem Oppiam abrogaritis.

The verb is complete future ; future because *erit* is future, complete future because antecedent in time to *erit*. The same account must be given of the tense of *volueritis* below, with this difference that *volueritis* is frequentative, i.e. *si* = " if ever."

you will be powerless

=non vestri arbitrii erit.

For the genitive see Roby, § 1282. The prepositive *vestri* has some stress and *non* qualifies it = " it will not be in *your* hands." Contrast the normal order *arbitrii vestri non erit*.

should you desire to enforce any prohibition now contained in that law !

=si quid eius vetare volueritis, quod nunc lex vetat.

Lit. " if you desire to forbid anything of that which now the law forbids."

The noun "prohibition" is expressed by a verb. There is stress on "now" as contrasted with the future ; *nunc*, therefore, is put early = νυνὶ δή.

Note the repetition *vetare... vetat*)(English.

For *lex* as subject to a transitive verb, see 34. 4. 13 on *utrumque lex vobis demit*.

Of course, our daughters, wives, and even sisters will be less under control in certain households !

= minus filiae, uxores, sorores etiam quibusdam in manu erunt.

Note the asyndeton and the stress on *minus* coming first and separated far from *in manu erunt*. It illustrates Latin love of putting the negative idea early.

The irony of *scilicet* still continues. The word "our" needs no representation. The pronoun *quibusdam* is dative of the possessor and masculine gender.

§ 12.   But never

= numquam.

Note the adversative asyndeton.

while their male relatives are living

= salvis suis.

If "men-folk" had reached the dignity of literary English, it would be the most convenient version of *suis*.

The ablative *salvis suis* is one of attendant circumstances.

For *salvus = incolumis = superstes* see Lewis and Short, s.v. *salvus* II. A.

The use of *suis* is due to the sense, as if Livy had written *liberae sunt mulieres*, instead of *exuitur servitus muliebris*.

is the yoke of slavery taken from women

= exuitur servitus muliebris.

The metaphor is from a yoke, cp. 35. 17. 8 *iugum exuere*, and 34. 13. 9 *se iugo exuere*. Thus *exuere* has the double meaning (1) "to get rid of," ἀπαλλάττειν τὸ ζυγόν ; (2) "to rid oneself of," ἀπαλλάττειν ἑαυτὸν τοῦ ζυγοῦ.

For the *tutela* of women see

and they themselves abhor the liberty which is brought by the loss of husband or father

Ramsay's *Antiquities*, p. 255 (Ramsay and Lanciani, p. 299).

= et ipsae libertatem, quam viduitas et orbitas facit, detestantur.

Here *ipsae* may suggest "when they are their own mistresses," cp. *ipse = dominus.*

The verb *facit* is singular number because *et* = "and as the case may be" = "or." Compare *que* = "or," and see note on 34. 1. 4, ad suadendum dissuadendumque.

For the phrase cp. 26. 41. 9 *orbitas ... frangit animum.* Livy has, however, no other examples of *orbitas* or *viduitas* as subjects to transitive verbs; but *facere*, like *movere*, is extremely common with abstract and non-personal subjects. See Appendix A.

§ 13. They desire that you, rather than the law, should regulate their adornment

= in vestro arbitrio suum ornatum quam in legis malunt esse.

Note (1) the absence of connective; (2) the prepositive *vestro*, preparing us for the antithesis *legis* (sc. *arbitrio*), and producing by somewhat artificial parallelism the prepositive *suum* : *you* are to control *their* adornment.

The position of *vestro* makes it = *vos* as subject. Compare *Pref.* § 5 (*malorum*) *quae nostra tot per annos vidit aetas*, where *nostra* = *nos ipsi.* See my note *ad loc.* in *Latin and English Idiom* (Camb. Univ. Press, 1909).

and you, on your part

        = et vos.

        Note that *vos* is emphatic because inserted = ὑμεῖς δέ)(αὐταὶ μὲν *ipsae* in § 12.

should have them under protection and guardianship, not hold them in bondage

        = in manu et tutela, non in servitio debetis habere eas.

        For *non* = "and not," "but not," see 34. 7. 6 (p. 183).

        Note the position of *eas*. Livy is fond of putting a single word after the verb, especially an iambus.

        Observe "have them under... hold them in...": English varies both verb and preposition; Latin has one verb and repeats the preposition.

preferring the title of father or husband to that of master.

        = et malle patres vos aut viros quam dominos dici.

        Lit. "and (you ought) to prefer...": Latin goes on with a parallel construction; English varies with a participle "preferring."

        The noun "title" > the verb *dici*. Observe the stress on *patres* preceding *vos* the subject of *dici*; and note the repetition *malunt...malle*)(English variety "they desire...rather,"... "preferring...."

§ 14.

        In the first sentence note (1) no connective; (2) stress on *invidiosis* prepositive = "producing hatred"; (3) the position of *consul*: our attention is drawn to his official standing, and we feel that more careful language might be expected from a responsible magistrate; (4) the order of *modo*, which is ἀπὸ κοινοῦ, like *consul*, with *utebatur* and *appellando*; (5) *appellando* — the Livian "modal gerund" = *appellans* = Greek instrumental participle.

when he talked of sedition and secession on the part of the women

= seditionem muliebrem et secessionem appellando.

Note the ἀπὸ κοινοῦ position of *muliebrem* between the two nouns.

The danger is that they may seize

= id enim periculum est, ne... capiant.

Note the connective and the anticipatory *id*.

The whole of this sentence is ironical. Latin usually *shows* irony by the insertion of *scilicet*, *sane*, etc. A few adjectives (e.g. *praeclarus*) are common in an ironical sense.

that they may seize the Sacred Hill—an angry plebs once did it —or perhaps the Aventine!

= ne Sacrum montem, sicut quondam irata plebs (sc. cepit), aut Aventinum capiant.

W. on 2. 32. 2 says that *Sacer mons* is the usual order. The Secession of the plebs is dated B.C. 494. The historian Calpurnius Piso (consul B.C. 133) asserted that the Secession was made to the Aventine.

The participle *irata* is prepositive because causal; it is more than a mere epithet. Greek would have ὀργιζόμενος ὁ δῆμος.

Note *aut* = "or perhaps." For this use of *aut* cp. *tres aut summum quattuor,* and see M. § 436.

§ 15.

Note the adversative asyndeton. The word *patiendum* comes early for stress. So far from acting with spirit and independence, these poor women must *submit.* Compare the position of *remissa* at 34. 8. 2.

no matter what you decide

= quodcumque vos censueritis.

Lit. "there must be endured whatever *you* (emphatic because *vos* is inserted) shall have decided."

The verb *censueritis* is future because *patiendum est = patientur mulieres,* and complete future because antecedent to the time of *patientur.*

It is worth while to remember that *faciet* may be represented by *facturus est, facturus erit,* and *fiet* by *faciendum est, faciendum erit.* See Roby, § 1520.

The verb *censere* is properly used of the Senate, and *iubere* of the *populus.* The latter is now being addressed, and we should expect *iubere.*

Yet the greater your power, the more moderate should be your exercise of it.

= quo plus potestis, eo moderatius imperio uti debetis.

Note no connective again. Lit. "by what (measure) you are more powerful, by that (measure) you ought to use authority more moderately."

The ablatives *quo...eo* are ablatives of measure of difference.

The *plus* of *plus potestis* is practically an adverb, although in origin an internal accusative, closely allied to the accusative of "extent over which."

Observe that the noun "exercise" > the verb (*uti* despite *utebatur* in § 14); contrast the English variety " (for a consul) to use"... "exercise (of it)."

CHAPTER VIII

§ 1. Such were the speeches made.... Crowds of women... poured...

= Haec cum...dicta essent,...frequentia mulierum...sese effudit.

Latin subordinates the first sentence. Perhaps *haec* is brought forward to express: "although *all this* had been said," i.e. although the case had been put so fully, the women did not desist from their agitation.

At the same time, Livy, not infrequently, puts the subject of the subordinate clause before the conjunction (here *cum*) even when it is not subject to the principal verb as well.

The noun "speeches" > verb *dicta essent.*

in favour of or against the law

= contra legem proque lege.

The noun is usually repeated in such cases, cp. 8. 11. 7, 29. 19. 10. But at 10. 7. 2 we have *pro lege contraque eam.* In two instances the second preposition stands alone, viz. 5. 35. 4 *cis Padum ultraque*, and 9. 32. 9 *ante signa circaque*; but it is noticeable that both *ultra* and *circa* are more adverbs than prepositions.

For "or"=*que* see on 34. 1. 4 ad suadendum dissuadendumque.

Crowds of women, in larger numbers than ever, poured next day into the streets

=aliquanto maior frequentia mulierum postero die sese in publicum effudit.

The first two words are predicative, "being by a considerable amount greater" = πολλῷ μείζων οὖσα ἡ σύνοδος τῶν γυναικῶν.

poured

=sese...effudit.

English has many of these quasi-intransitive verbs with the reflexive object omitted, e.g. pour, move, burn, drive, turn, etc. Latin and Greek have very few. Compare, however, *terra movet*, ἐλαύνει (he drives, rides), ὁρμᾷ (he advances).

The *sese* is thrown in neatly between the two adverbs.

For *in publicum* cp. 34. 5. 7, and note on 34. 2. 10 *in publico*.

The word *frequentia* occurs only twice elsewhere in Livy as subject to a transitive verb, viz. 2. 1. 10 and 7. 30. 21. In the first passage the object is non-personal, in the second no object is expressed. See Appendix A.

§ 2.   A mass meeting

=unoque agmine omnes.

Note the connective *que*, and

the artificial sound of *uno...omnes*. This antithesis is dear to the ancients. Thus "He did it all by himself"= unus omnia egit, εἰς πάντα ἐποίησεν. Compare 34. 9. 3. "To-day all are fused together into one body politic"=nunc in corpus unum confusi omnes, where the abnormally postpositive *unum*, and the *omnes* placed after the verb, serve to heighten the antithesis.

besieged the doors of the Bruti = Brutorum ianuas obsederunt.

The prepositive genitive is the important word. The Bruti (Marcus and Publius Junius) were opposed to their colleagues. See 34. 1. 4.

Note that *ianua*=gate of a house=ἡ θύρα)(porta=gate of a city=αἱ πύλαι.

who were attempting to block their colleagues' proposal = qui collegarum rogationi intercedebant.

The imperfect *intercedebant* is conative. The genitive *collegarum* is prepositive because the *Bruti* were opposing their *colleagues*, cp. the prepositive *Brutorum* above.

The position of this relative clause is awkward. It should stand between *Brutorum* and *ianuas*. There is a reading *tribunorum* (for *Brutorum*), and, perhaps, the anticipatory *eorum* has dropped out before it. Then *Brutorum* would be an explanatory gloss (on *tribunorum*) which has crept into the text.

The women persisted in these methods

=nec ante abstiterunt.

Note the connective *nec*=*et non*, and the anticipatory order of *ante* preparing us for *quam*.

Latin continues the original construction (parallelism); English varies with a new subject (women).

until opposition was abandoned by the tribunes

=(ante)...quam remissa intercessio ab tribunis est.

Note the stress on *remissa* coming first and separated from *est*. Compare 34. 5. 9 *obruta... redempta*.

When the principal sentence is negative, Livy rarely writes anything but the indicative (usually aorist perfect) after the *quam*. See W.'s note on 23. 30. 4.

§ 3.   There was then no doubt

=nulla deinde dubitatio fuit.

The *nulla* has stress by separation, cp. οὐδὲ εἷς for the less emphatic οὐδείς. The adverb *deinde* not seldom comes second.

that the Lex Oppia would be repealed by all the tribes

=quin omnes tribus legem abrogarent.

The construction is as if with *nullus fuit metus ne non....*

Thus " I do not doubt that he *will come*" may be expressed by *non dubito quin ille veniat*, as if *non timeo ne non ille veniat*.

But Cicero, *Fam.* 2. 17. 5, has the periphrastic future: *nunc mihi non est dubium quin venturae non sint* (*legiones*), where the method of expression is perhaps due to the preceding words, *antea dubitabam venturaene essent legiones.*

A good instance of the present subjunctive (=periphrastic future) after a verb of doubt is Caes. *B. G.* 1. 31. 15 (*dixit se*) *non dubitare quin...supplicium sumat* (=*sumpturus sit*) *Ariovistus.*

and repealed it was twenty years after it first became law

=viginti annis post abrogata est quam lata.

Note no connective.

For the facts and construction see 34. 6. 9 on *viginti ante annis latam* (p. 152).

Note the anticipatory position of *post* preparing us for *quam.*

APPENDIX A

On 34. 2. 8. quod nisi me verecundia...tenuisset.

Latin, we are told, is a language of concrete expressions, and it is startling to come across such phrases as *hae spes Etruscos armaverant* (2. 44. 12), *plebem ira prope armavit* (2. 35. 1), *cum timor par adversus communem hostem duas...urbes armaret* (9. 19. 13). When we learn that Livy has some 1690 examples no less bold, i.e. more than 48 in each of the extant books, we may well begin to wonder if the old canon needs revision or modification.

The following pages are the result of a painful investigation. Space will not permit detailed references, and the reader is asked to take the figures on trust.

There are in Livy some 4375 instances (to which 814 nouns contribute) of non-personal or abstract subjects to transitive verbs. In 406 cases the verb is either intransitively used or the object is so vague as to make the verb practically intransitive.

The remaining 3969 may be divided thus: (*a*) words containing abstract ideas or denoting inanimate entities; (*β*) words of a collective nature* or words which imply living persons, such as *exercitus, navis, multitudo, civitas*, etc. Of class (*a*) there are 3109 examples (i.e. more than 88 in each of the extant books); of class (*β*) there are 860.

Of class (*a*) more than half the examples, viz. 1690, are purely abstract in sense; and of them 756 have a *person* as object, and 934 a *thing*. Of the 756 examples where the object is a *person*, 435 have the *subject* before the object and verb, while 321 have the *object* before the subject and verb; that is, 435 are of the type *necessitas me cogit*, and 321 of the type *me necessitas cogit*.

Of the 934 examples where the object is a *thing*, 714 have the *subject* before the object and verb, while 220 only have the *object* before the

* I do not include *senatus* and *plebes*.

subject and verb; that is, 714 are of the type *cura animum incessit*, and 220 of the type *animum cura incessit*.

*In my statistics I shall call the type *necessitas me cogit* A^1, and *me necessitas cogit* A^2; while I shall call the type *cura animum incessit* B^1, and *animum cura incessit* B^2.

Thus A^1 is to A^2 as 1·36 to 1 ($A^1=435$, $A^2=321$), whereas B^1 is to B^2 as 3·25 to 1 ($B^1=714$, $B^2=220$); and we deduce the important fact that, when the subject is purely abstract, if the object be *personal*, Livy puts it before the subject *thrice* out of *seven* examples, but if the object be *non-personal*, he puts it before the subject *thrice* only in *thirteen* examples. That is to say, the type *me necessitas cogit* occurs three times to four of *necessitas me cogit*, whereas the type *animum cura incessit* occurs three times to ten of *cura animum incessit*.

In striking contrast stand the figures of class (β), i.e. words of a collective nature and words which imply living persons. These figures are $A^1=200$, $A^2=65$, $B^1=530$, $B^2=65$; and we note that as the subject more nearly approaches genuine personality, Livy takes less trouble to bring the personal object before the subject; for the relation of A^1 to A^2 is now 3·08 to 1, whereas with purely abstract subjects it was 1·36 to 1. As for B^1 and B^2, the relation is 8·15 to 1, whereas with purely abstract subjects it was 3·25 to 1.

The following table gives a conspectus of results:—

Abstract Nouns

$A^1=436$, $A^2=320$	Total 756 ⎫ = 1690	$A^1 : A^2 :: 1·36 : 1$
$B^1=714$, $B^2=220$	Total 934 ⎭	$B^1 : B^2 :: 3·25 : 1$

Abstract and Inanimate Entities

$A^1= 668$, $A^2=461$	Total 1129 ⎫ = 2758	$A^1 : A^2 :: 1·44 : 1$
$B^1=1297$, $B^2=332$	Total 1629 ⎭	$B^1 : B^2 :: 3·90 : 1$

Abstract and Inan. Entities+res *and neuters*

$A^1= 768$, $A^2=493$	Total 1261 ⎫ = 3109	$A^1 : A^2 :: 1·55 : 1$
$B^1=1488$, $B^2=360$	Total 1848 ⎭	$B^1 : B^2 :: 4·13 : 1$

Words implying living persons (*e.g.* civitas, *etc.*)

$A^1=200$, $A^2=65$	Total 265 ⎫ = 860	$A^1 : A^2 :: 3·08 : 1$
$B^1=530$, $B^2=65$	Total 595 ⎭	$B^1 : B^2 :: 8·15 : 1$

I append a list of the most common abstract and non-personal nouns. The letter C denotes that the verb is used absolutely or with so vague an object as to make the verb practically absolute, or, again, to denote that a transitive verb is used intransitively.

* The few relative clauses I have classed under A^1 and B^1.

	A¹, A², B¹, B², C	Total

i. Abstract

Fortuna	10, 22, 54, 27, 10	= 123
Fama	10, 8, 17, 5, 12	= 52
Bellum	14, 7, 14, 6, 3	= 44
Metus	17, 8, 12, 2, 5	= 44
Terror	11, 10, 15, 3, 3	= 42
Spes	13, 6, 13, 2, 5	= 39
Ira	7, 9, 13, 4, 6	= 39
Cura	8, 12, 7, 3, 7	= 37
Pavor	15, 8, 9, 4, 0	= 36
Vis	7, 4, 9, 6, 3	= 29
Adventus	6, 2, 13, 5, 1	= 27
Timor	11, 2, 10, 1, 3	= 27
Virtus	4, 3, 10, 3, 5	= 25
Causa	9, 6, 7, 2, 0	= 24
Mors	5, 3, 7, 4, 2	= 21
Pudor	5, 6, 7, 0, 3	= 21
Religio	4, 8, 1, 3, 4	= 20
Clades	5, 1, 8, 3, 2	= 19
Casus	5, 2, 8, 1, 1	= 17
Fuga	7, 0, 8, 2, 0	= 17
Impetus	5, 5, 6, 0, 0	= 16
Necessitas	3, 4, 6, 1, 2	= 16

ii. Natural Phenomena

Tempus	4, 2, 15, 4, 14*	= 39
Nox	6, 7, 24, 1, 0	= 38
Tempestas	6, 4, 13, 5, 1	= 29
Annus	9, 6, 4, 3, 1	= 23
Dies	5, 2, 11, 1, 0	= 19
Ventus	2, 3, 8, 2, 4	= 19
Lux	2, 2, 10, 0, 2	= 16

iii. Geographical

Amnis	2, 3, 21, 2, 4	= 32
Locus	7, 3, 9, 1, 11†	= 31
Via	1, 1, 0, 0, 16‡	= 18

iv. Bodily functions and parts

Clamor	11, 2, 23, 3, 3	= 42
Animus	3, 3, 17, 3, 2	= 28
Vox	6, 1, 14, 1, 3	= 25
Vires	6, 3, 6, 0, 1	= 16

v. Legal and Parliamentary

Lex	8, 1, 15, 2, 3	= 29
Sententia	8, 7, 2, 0, 12§	= 29
Oratio	7, 4, 4, 3, 1	= 19

vi. Concrete

Litterae	7, 1, 12, 3, 3	= 26
Nomen	4, 1, 7, 2, 1	= 15

vii. Res and neuters

Res	37, 15, 89, 24, 38‖	= 203
Quod (=thing which)	20, 2, 21, 0, 3	= 46
Id	11, 0, 16, 0, 2	= 29
Hoc	5, 0, 18, 0, 2	= 25
Quod (=fact that)	5, 5, 5, 3, 6	= 24

viii. Collective and quasi-personal

Exercitus	18, 3, 43, 8, 3	= 75
Navis	5, 1, 57, 3, 7	= 73
Populus	18, 7, 35, 10, 1	= 71
Multitudo	19, 8, 33, 2, 3	= 65
Civitas	18, 2, 33, 5, 3	= 61
Legio	9, 1, 30, 3, 0	= 43
Gens	14, 1, 20, 1, 3	= 39
Pars	5, 1, 27, 1, 5	= 39
Urbs	7, 5, 19, 3, 1	= 35
Acies	11, 3, 12, 3, 4	= 33
Classis	5, 0, 25, 3, 0	= 33
Oppidum	2, 1, 11, 1, 0	= 15

* Mostly *ut tempus patitur, ut tempus postulat.*
† Mostly *ut locus patitur, postulat.*   ‡ Mostly *via fert.*
§ 11 of *sententia vincit.*
‖ Mostly with *poscit, postulat.*

VERBS.

Livy has some 621 transitive verbs with non-personal and abstract subjects. I append a list of those that occur most frequently. It will be noticed that the first eight verbs, if we include compounds (*efficere, adferre, accipere, excipere, continere, inferre, prohibere*), account for not much less than one-third of the examples, viz. 1340 out of 4375.

	No. of times		No. of times		No. of times		No. of times
facere	323	sequi	53	tegere	30	turbare	23
habere	208	impedire	40	accipere	29	urgere	23
movere	127	augere	39	incessere	29	vertere	23
tenere	127	stimulare	39	pati	29	claudere	22
dare	98	efficere	36	trahere	28	opprimere	22
ferre	93	excitare	35	adiuvare	26	poscere	22
capere	89	terrere	35	occupare	25	postulare	21
praebere	89	adferre	34	absumere	24	inferre	20
cogere	67	fallere	33	excipere	24	prohibere	20
vincere	56	dirimere	32	invadere	24		
avertere	54	accendere	31	continere	23		

APPENDIX B

On 34. 3. 7. sed tamen, cum fuit, negastis hoc.

Weissenborn and Müller on Livy 1. 1. 1 have gathered many references illustrating the abnormal use of perfect for pluperfect and *vice versa*. I append a list of the examples that I have been able to discover, but do not repeat those contained in my note on 34. 3. 7.

(*a*) Perfect for pluperfect in subordinate clause.

1. 1. 1. constat duobus...quia pacis...auctores fuerunt (Madv. fuerant)...ius belli Achivos abstinuisse.

2. 30. 15. paucis dată veniă, qui inermes in deditionem venerunt (cp. Caes. *B. C.* 3. 18. 5 ab iis...cognovit, qui sermoni interfuerunt).

39. 31. 18. donati et centuriones..., maxime qui mediam aciem tenuerunt.

3. 24. 11. consulum magna...gloria fuit, quod et foris pacem peperere, et domi...minus...infesta civitas fuit.

4. 51. 8. minus praedae...fuit, quod Volsci...oppidum reliquerunt (W. reliquerant).

9. 21. 4. tutam aciem dictator habuit, quia...locum haud facilem... cepit.

10. 33. 4. impulsos semel terrore eodem, quo coeperunt (Madv. coeperant) expellunt. (But the historic present of the main verb makes *coeperunt* possible.)

25. 29. 9. ad caedem...discurrunt quosque fors obtulit, irati interfecere (P. interficere) atque omnia, quae in promptu erant, diripuerunt.

39. 28. 5. pro non dubio...legati Eumenis sumebant, quae Antiochi fuerunt, Eumenem aequius esse quam me habere.

36. 39. 10. (censebat § 6)...P. Cornelium multorum exemplo, qui in magistratu non triumphaverunt, triumphaturum esse.

43. 13. 8. omnia, uti decemviri praeierunt, facta.

5. 8. 13. pauci rei publicae...ut quosque studium...aut gratia occupaverunt, adsunt. W. reads occupaverat. The tense, but not the number, of *occupaverunt* might stand as a complete present.

37. 43. 8. postremos, ut quosque adepti sunt, caedunt. Here *adepti sunt* might be a complete present.

10. 44. 4. Papirium propter navatam...in proelio operam et nocte, qua fugam infestam Samnitibus fecit,...donat.

32. 26. 3. cum duos exercitus in provincia habuisset, unum retentum, quem dimitti oportebat..., alterum, quem in provinciam adduxit, totum prope annum...consumpsit.

39. 23. 9. quia iussus abscedere...erat, Romanisque oppidum deditum est, aegre eam rem tulerat.

34. 13. 1. consul, ubi satis, quod in speciem fuit, ostentatum est, revocari ex navibus milites iubet. Compare Caes. *B. G.* 1. 51. 1.

    (b)   Perfect for pluperfect in the principal clause and *vice versa*.

10. 12. 5. lux insequens victorem victumque ostendit ; nam Etrusci... castra reliquerunt (W. desiderates *reliquerant*).

24. 43. 3. dimissique fuerant. (Ussing omits *fuerant*. Others read *fuerunt*.)

    (c) *(1)*   Pluperfect in one sentence followed by an aorist perfect in the next, or *(2)* *vice versa*.

For (1) cp. 2. 1. 2, 9. 22. 2 (most MSS. *posuerunt*. W. reads *posuerant*), 28. 22. 4, 21. 8. 5 (MSS. *prociderunt*. W. *prociderant*), 41. 4. 4, 38. 26. 3 (MSS. *locaverunt*. Madv. *locaverant*), 2. 19. 7, 26. 37. 2, 42. 7. 8, 9. 46. 11.

For (2) cp. 42. 51. 5, 27. 39. 13, 23. 29. 16, 4. 20. 3. (This last is really an instance of the "instantaneous pluperfect." Cp. 1. 12. 10, 2. 5. 6, 32. 12. 3, etc., and see Roby, § 1492.) At 29. 2. 5 we have an imperfect followed by a perfect *fecerunt* (but W. reads *fecerant*).

I may be allowed to add three examples of *postquam* followed by varying moods and tenses in the same sentence, viz. 4. 13. 10 quae postquam sunt audita, et (W. cum) undique primores...increparent (compare 30. 44. 10 where *cum* is followed first by the indicative and then by the subjunctive); 6. 30. 7 postquam...res...adferebatur et apparuit...; 7. 2. 11 postquam...ab risu ac soluto ioco res avocabatur et ludus in artem paulatim verterat.... Here *paulatim* makes the pluperfect necessary, for if the time occupied by the *postquam* clause is lengthy, the aorist perfect is impossible. For Livy's varying use with *biduo quo*, etc. see W. on 3. 8. 2 and 40. 53. 1.

W. also quotes 9. 25. 5 and 37. 34. 6, in both of which passages an unexpected perfect indicative occurs (according to the MSS.) in Or. Obl. Finally at 24. 7. 2 we have *cum...profectus erat* for *profectus esset*.

It should be noted that with *quamdiu* the perfect is always used where the main verb is perfect, and that with *dum* (= all the time that) or *quoad* either perfect or imperfect is used where the main verb is perfect or pluperfect.

INDEX

References are to pages. b = *bottom of page;* t = *top of page.*

A principio + iam 127
Ablative of attendant circumstances
    49 b, 189
  causal 181 b, 186
  in -*e* and -*i* 123, 125, 136
  of measure of difference 85, 152,
    193 b, 195, 198
  of time duration 144
  of time within which 165
  to turn abstract subject of English
    72, 128 (cp. 130, 131), 154
Abrogare 151
Abstinere ± *ab* 76
Abstract nouns ; *see also* "Infinitive"
)(concrete expressions of Latin
    31, 41, 52, 61, 119, 152
  plural of 29, 87 t
  subjects to transitive verbs App.
    A, **54**, **55**, 59, 80, 92, 94 (bis),
    96 t, 101, 145 (bis), 147, 155,
    156, 160, 166, 188 b, 190, 195
  subjects turned by
    ablative 72, 128, 154 (cp. 130, 131)
    gerundive 124, 140, 163
    participle 156 t
Ac subdividing *et...et* 123 ; *see*
  "Aut," "Ve," "Que"
Accidere)(contingere 185
Accipere = audire 126
  in bonam partem 113 t
  leges 53
Accurata -ior oratio 117 t
Accusative -*is* for -*es* 39, 89 t, 112 t,
  136
  internal 184, 194 t
  of distance away 35
  of exclamation 105 b

Adjectives ; *see* ORDER and
  "Neuter"
  combined with relative + subjunc-
    tive 28
  of English = adverbs of Latin 41,
    44, 85, 92, 127
  of Latin = nouns of English 58,
    76, 97, 118 b, 121, 126, 132,
    134, 142 t, 161, 195
  of locality come first 128 t
  possessive as antecedent ; *see*
    "Nostra"
  two without connective 149
Admovere exercitum, machinam 157
Adverbs; *see* ORDER
  carelessly placed in English 136
    (cp. 115, 116)
  of English > adjectives of Latin
    46
  of Latin > adjectives of English
    41, 44, 85, 92, 127
    = preposition + demonstrative of
    English 36 t
Adversative; *see* "Asyndeton"
Aequo animo 64
Aerarium 161
"Again" = quid? = καὶ μήν, τί δέ; 129
Agent, dative of 134
Agitur 138
Agmen)(turba 54
Aiebat with obscure subject 179;
  see "Inquit"
Aio with *neque...neque* 36
ἀκράτεια = impotentia 47
ἀκρατής = impotens 63
"Alias ornate" 46, 119, 125
Alii for *ceteri* 170 t; *see* "Alius"
Aliquis prepositive 143, 145 (bis)

Alius ullus 95; *see* "Alii," and "Quid aliud"

"All of whom" 84

ἀλλὰ νὴ Δία; *see* "At"

ἀλλ' οὐ=nec 134

Alter)(unus 43 t

Ambiguous gender 67, 109

An)(aut 149; in questions 58

Anaphora; *see* "Rhetorical devices," 63 t, 83, 157, 162, 182 t, 187 t (cp. 82)
  with change of case (πολύπτωτον) 186

"And," variety of words for in Latin 83, 86

"And...he"=qui; *see* "Relative"

"And...not"=non 119, 183, 191

"And then"=deinde 110

"And therefore," how to translate 47, 74, 150, 153, 175

Animus iniquus 64
  to be omitted in English 91

Annon 50

Antecedent; *see also* "Relative" and "Nostra"
  drawn into relative clause 84
  of English following relative clause in Latin 71, 75 b, 135, 145

Antefixa 89

Antequam with indicative after negative princ. clause 197
  with subjunctive 109

Anticipatory words: *ante* 93, 197; *aut* 64, 99, 167; *ea* 148, 181; *eam* 140 t; *eorum* 64; *et...et* 109, 132, 139, 179; *id* 73 b, 104 (=only), 192; *ideo* 155; *iis* 142; *illum* 106 t; *ita* omitted 163 t, anticipatory of *si* 90; *magis, plus* etc. 87, 120 b; *post* 198; *prius* 93; *tam* 166; *tum* 95; *vel* 100

"Antiquities" of Cato 126

Antiquus)(novus 70;)(vetus 154 b

Antitheses, artificial 73, 196 t; *see also* "Rhetorical"

Aorist Perfect; *see* "Perfect"

Apodosis; *see also* "Subjunctive"
  in the infinitive 69
  resolved forms of 103, 114
  tenses of 75
  to be supplied 64 t

ἀπὸ κοινοῦ; *see* ORDER

Argentum factum, infectum, signatum 162

Arguere 144

Article definite=is, ille 130

Artificial antitheses; *see* "Antitheses"

Asia=Asia Minor 86

Asyndeton; *see also* "Connectives"
  Adversative 39 t, 48, 51, 53, 61, 63, 69, 71 (word of positive meaning supplied; *see* "Sed"), 73, 97, 107, 111, 119, 134, 170, 173 t, 178 b, 182, 185, 189, 193 t
  Bi-membral 31, 61, 72, 136, 152, 171, 176
  in English and Latin 148 t
  of two or more adjectives 149
  with relatives 147

At=at enim=ἀλλὰ νὴ Δία 70 t, 79 b
  +hercule 70 t, 180

Atque 49, 97, 187

Attendant circumstances expressed by preposition *in* 31, 123 t, 136, 146 b, 147, 187 (bis)

Attracted subjunctive; *see* "Subjunctive"

Attraction of *hic* to gender of nearest word 186

Aures occupare 137
  superbae 137

Aurum factum, infectum, signatum 162

Aut: aut...aut)(vel...vel 64
  following *nec* 185 (*see* "Ve")
  for *neve* 34
  in questions)(an 149
  ="or at any rate" 155
  ="or perhaps" 192 b
  subdivided by *vel...vel* 35 (*see* "Ac," "Que," "Ve")
  to carry on a negative 98
  with *aut* subdividing an original negative 38, cp. 185

αὐτὰ δείξει 156

Autem third 156

Auxiliary in indicative 184 (*see* "Esse")
  +infinitive = subjunctive 60
  separated from participle 140

Believing, verbs of early; *see* "Showing"

Bellum, subject to transitive verb 147 (*see* "Abstract")
Bestiae 110
Bi-membral; *see* "Asyndeton"
Bonam in partem accipere 113 t
Bono publico 127 t
"Book, to open, close" 126
Brevity of Latin 51, 52 b; *see* "Ornament"
Bruti 36, 196; *see* "Proper Names"
"But if (not)" 54
"But not" = non 119, 183, 191

C = Gaius 31
Caligatus 172 t
Calpurnius Piso 192
Carelessness of English in regard to the position of the negative 115 b, 116 t, cp. 136
Case-endings, value of 51
Case-relations grouped together 57, 77 t, 84, 89, 137
Cato's "Antiquities" 126
Causa, subject to transitive verb 92; *see* "Abstract"
"Cause of," how to translate 156
Cautum in lege 161
Censere 110 b;)(iubere 193
Cereris sacrificium 164
Cerneres 111 b
Ceterum 43, 135
Ceteri, *alii* used for 170 t
Chiasmus; *see* ORDER
χρήμασι πείθειν 91
Cincian Law 95
Cineas 91 t
Circumstances; *see* "Attendant"
Civitas)(patria, respublica 77
Classem tueri 158
"Close a book" 126
"Coals to Newcastle" 58 t
Coarguere 144
Coepi)(incipio 95
Coloniae 172
Complement outside
  when a complement has already occurred inside 32
  when genitive with noun forms one phrase 39
  when noun is emphatic 177 b
  when preposition occurs 31, 32, 54, 159

Complement outside when still awaited by sense of preceding word 32
  within 86 b, 94, 99, 102, 113, 139 t, 150, 160, 172
Conative imperfect 44, 91 (Greek), 96, 196
  present 149 t
Concessive; *see* "Subjunctive"
Conciliabula 43
Concord; *see* "Neuter"
Concrete; *see* "Abstract"
Conditionals; *see* "Apodosis," and "Subjunctive"
Conducere + gerundive 160, 168
Connectives; *see* "Anaphora," "Asyndeton," "Que"
  absence of 37, 38, 54, 64 b, 73, 75 t, 77, 95, 104, 112 (whole of Chap. IV), 121 t, 122, 123, 126 (bis), 131 b, 134, 137, 138, 140, 146, 157 t, 170 t, 171, 183 b, 185, 187, 190, 191, 193, 198
  inserted 82, 95, 98, 154, 175, 176, 192, 195 b, 197 t
  omitted in Livy's short sentence style 42
  omitted in series 37, 62 t, 189
  or all inserted 49, 57, 108, 121, 186
  relative as 44, 50, 67, 117, 152
  repeated negative as 82 b
  repeated phrase as 83, 182 t, 187
  repeated preposition as 82
  repeated verb as 30
Consecution; *see* "Subordinate Clause"
Consecutive; *see* "Ut"
Consensu ± omnium 131
Consularis 140
Consul, order of in sentence 138, 191 b
Consuls, names of ± *et* 31
Contemnere)(despicere 104
Contineri, construction of 38, 60
Contingere)(accidere 185
Continuare 94
Continuus 94
Contrasts artificial; *see* "Rhetorical Devices"
Copula omitted where *quo...eo* occur 85
Corrective *et* 96

Cotidie 41, 85; *see* "Dies"
Crede mihi 88
"Crowds"=turba 37; *see* "Agmen"
Cultus 186 t
Cum=ἐπεί=γάρ 106
   clause of abnormally preceded by subject 148 and 194
   +indicative=*quod* 96 t, 101, 106, 180
Cunctus 133, 180; without preposition 128 t
Cupido, subject to transitive verb 94; *see* "Abstract"
   Cicero's use of 94
Curro, compounds of 76
Cybele, cult of 80

Darkness; *see* "Metaphor"
Dash of English translated by genitive 56
Data et oblata 96
Dative of agent 134
   ethical 69
   of person interested or judging 58
   predicative 147
De in *defero, descendo*, etc. 161
Dead metaphor; *see* "Metaphor"
"Dear Marcus," order of in Latin 45
Decuit + infinitive 59, 60
Definite Article=*is, ille* 130
Deinde="and then" 110
   coming second 197
δείξει αὐτά 156
Demonstrative between interrogative and noun 56
Dependent Jussive, etc.; *see* "Subjunctive"
   Questions; *see* "Indicative," "Perfect," and "Subjunctive"
Despicere)(contemnere 104
Dicere leges 53
   vere 65
Dictu; *see* "Supine"
Dies, gender of 159
   in dies 41, 42, 85, 86 t
Different pronouns for the same person 182
Difficile est 105
Diis placet; *see* "Si"
Dimicari 127
Diminutives 184
Dissuadere legem 37, 113 b, 118

Doublets, rhetorical 47; *see* "Rhetorical"
Doubting, construction with words of 197
Dubitare, construction with 197
Dubium est, construction with 197
Ducere omits *esse* 48
Dumtaxat 174
Duration of time expressed by ablative 144
δώροις πείθειν 91

E, ex expresses completion 187
   ="in" of English 80
   ="in accordance with" 50, 160
   -*e* for -*i*; *see* "Ablative"
"Ear, to gain" 137
Earum for *sui* 77
Eas for *se* 70
ἔχει="involves" 98
Effundi + *in, ad* 154
Egestas 100 b
Ego inserted for emphasis 49, 89, 97, 111 t, 142
ἔγωγε, ἐγὼ μέν 97
Egregium publicum 127 t
Emphasis; *see* ORDER
   awkward methods of expressing in English 65, 80, 101, 107
Eo picking up *quo* 85
ἐπεί=cum=γάρ 106
ἐφορᾶν=videre 181
Epistulam reddere 168
Equidem 48, 54 t
Erat)(fuit 92 b
Error 141
ἔς="up to the time of," "against" 159 b
Esse, omission of 48 (with *duco*), 63, 109 t, 112, 134
"Essential to," how translated 151
Est + facile, par, etc. 105
Et="or" 190; *see* "Que"
   et...et; *see* "Anticipatory"
   et...et=ut...ita 109
   et...etiam 87
   et corrective or explanatory 96
   et...quidem 118, 126 b
   et...quoque 62
Etiam; *see* "Et"
Ex; *see* "E"
Exaggeration of Latin superlative 115 t

Excedere + *in* 29
Exclamation, accusative of 105 b
ἐξελέγχειν 144
Exemplum 49
Existimare 50
Existimarint, form of 151
Existimatio 50
Exorabilis = παραιτητός 107 b
Explanatory; *see* "Et," and "Ut"
Expugnare in metaphor 66
Extemplo followed by *simul* 69
Exuere, constructions of 189

Facere inserted or omitted with *quid aliud* 62, 187
   "vicarious" 169
   with abstract subject 145, 190
Facile est 105
Factum aurum 162
"Failed to," translation of 48 t
Familias + pater 45, 175
Faxo 111
"Feeling of shame, vexation" 99
Ferre rogationem)(legem 30
Final clause, order of 133 b
Fires; *see* "Metaphor"
"Firstly...secondly" = et...et 139
"Foot, on" 182
Fora 43
Foret, use of 155
Formality of Latin; *see* " Variety," 38, 43, 106, 124 t, 142, 147 (in a simile)
"Former...latter" 140
Fortuna, plural of 41, 161; *see* App. A
Frenum 63
Frequentative; *see* "Imperfect"
Frequentia, subject to transitive verb 195; *see* "Abstract"
Fulgēre 81
"Furthermore" = iam 130
Future; *see* "Subordinate Clause"
   future perfect of *pudere* 105 ; of Recta > Pluperfect of Subjunctive 167
   periphrastic for simple future where the principal clause is present 51
   resolved equivalents of 193
   tense fixed by tense of the principal clause 75, 105, 106, 108, 111, 141, 188, 193

"Gain ear of" 137
Gaius = C 31
γάρ = cum = ἐπεί 106
Gaza 87
Gender ambiguous 67, 109
Genitive; *see* "Plebi"
   double 56, 181 t
   of definition = dash of English 56
   objective 45, 55
   partitive 45, 46, 142 ; *see* ORDER
   prepositive ; *see* ORDER
   separated for emphasis 56 ; *see* ORDER
   subjective 27, 179
   translated by prepositional phrase in English 39, 55, 65, 86, 92, 94, 97, 165, 167 t, 171 t, 173, 177, 179
"Gentlemen," position of in Latin 44, 103
Genus, meanings of 48
Gerere)(gestare 82
Gerund = Greek instrumental participle 73
   Livian modal = present participle 192
   in -*iundi* 92
   + *est* = future 193
   + "without," how translated 120
   with preposition may govern only a neuter pronoun 118
Gerundive = abstract noun of English 124, 140, 163
   + *locare, conducere, curare* 160, 168
Gestare)(gerere 82
Gladiator rudem 58 t
"Grounds of," how to translate 156
Grouping of case relations 57, 77 t, 84, 89

Habet = "involves" = ἔχει 98
Haec, referring to things of different genders 186
   subject to transitive verb 184
   = " these modern " 84
Haud (dubie) 52
Hendiadys 163, 180
Hercule ; *see* "At hercule "
Hexameter ending 60, 68, 185
Hic ; *see* "Haec," and "Demonstrative"

Hic attracted to gender of nearest word 186
= *talis* 102, 104 t
hic...ille = latter...former 140
hic and *ille* of the same person 182
Hoc, subject to transitive verb 184
Homo)(vir 115 t
Honestus 81
"Hopes" = spes (singular) 47
ὅσιος 82 t
Hostilis 81
ὑπάρχειν -οντα 179 t
Hypotheticals; *see* "Apodosis," and "Subjunctive"

I; *see* "Ablative"
Iacere aliquid = "level as a charge" 120
Iam = "actually," "really" 53
= "furthermore" and "already" 43
= "furthermore" = καὶ μήν 130
+ a principio 127
Ianua)(porta 196
Ideal Second Person = *tibi* 98, cp. 49
Ideo; *see* "Anticipatory"
Ille...hic = former...latter 140
used of same person 182
with *is* = definite article 130
Imperative, infinitive for in Greek 159
Imperfect; *see* "Subjunctive"
Conative 44, 91 (Greek), 96, 196
Frequentative 38, 42 b
Panoramic 42 b
Perfect contrasted 92 b
Impersonal use of *dimicare* 127
Impetrare 107
Impotens = ἀκρατής 63
Impotentia = ἀκράτεια 47
In = "in the case of" 45, 147, 178
= "up to the time of" 159 b; *see* "Dies"
expressing attendant circumstances 31, 123 t, 136, 146 b, 147 b, 187 (bis)
inserted or omitted with *loco* 108
not required 34 b
of English translated by *ex* or *in* + accusative 80
with *bonam partem* 113 t
with *utilis* 175

In with *eandem sententiam* 112
Incipio)(coepi 95
Incolumis 189
Indefinity in Latin expressions of time 54
Indicative; *see* "Subjunctive"
cum with; *see* "Cum"
for subjunctive in indignant questions 102
in dependent questions 74
in Oratio Obliqua 143
of auxiliary = subjunctive 60, 184
Indignant questions; *see* "Indicative"
Indignari 138, 139
Indignatio 99
Infectum aurum 162
Infensus 88
Inferre signa, play on 88
Infestus 88
Infinitive for imperative in Greek 159
subject to transitive verb 98; *see* "Abstract"
Iniquo animo 64
Inire rationem 98
Inopia, subject to transitive verb 166; *see* "Abstract"
Inquit; *see* "Aiebat"
vague subject of 81, 101
Instituere, meanings of 45
Instratus 176
Intercedere 27
Interdicere, construction of 174 b, 175 t
Interest sua, etc. 50, 51,)(ipsius
Internal accusative 184, 194
Intertrimentum 178
Intransitive verbs of English)(Latin 195
"Involves" = habet, ἔχει 98
Ipse = dominus 190
Ipsius with *interest*)(sua 50, 51
Irony, how shown in Latin 192
Is; *see* "Earum," "Eas"
= talis 181
= the definite article 130, cp. "Ille"
-is for *-es* 89 t, 112 t, 136
Iste to express sneer 58, 152, 155, 166
"It seems that")(personal expression of Latin 103, 157

Ita, anticipatory of *si* 90
   immediately preceding *ut* 158 b,
   159 ; *see* "Ut"
Iubere)(censere 193
Iuncto vehiculo ± equis 34, 35
-*iundi*, Gerund in 92
Iura = "limited rights" 66, cp.
   "Mos"
Ius)(leges 70

Jussive ; *see* "Subjunctive"

καί = *quoque* 133
καὶ μήν = *iam* 130
   = *quid* 129
καιρός = *tempus* 168
καίτοι = *quamquam* 58 b
κατά = "in accordance with" 160
καταφρονεῖν 104
Knowing, verbs of come early 37, 69,
   124 t, 142 (cp. 146, 179)

Latifundia 94
Latini nominis socii 181
"Latter...former" 140
Lex as subject to transitive verb 94 t,
   96 t, 101, 155, 188 ; *see* "Ab-
   stract"
   Cincia 95
   Licinia 94
   Oppia 152 ; *see* "Oppian"
   + accipere 53
   + dicere 53
   + ferre 30
   + rogare 107
   + suadere 37, 113 b, 118
   lege cautum 161
   leges)(ius 70
   leges, meaning of 53 b
Liberi)(pueri 108, 172
Libertas ; *see* "Liberties"
Liberties = libertas 47, cp. "Hopes"
Libertinus)(libertus 108, 172
Licentia 63
Licinian Law 94
Limiting *ut* 120
Locality, adjectives expressing come
   first 128 t
Locare + gerundive 160, 168
Loco ± *in* 108
Logical subject ; *see* "Subject"
Longum est 105

Luctus 164
Lugere 164
Luxuria 82
Luxus 82

Magna verba 123
Malignitas 178
Malo publico 127 t
Manupretium 178
Mater familiae 45, 175
Mĕdius, order of 127 b
   without preposition 128 t
Mēdius fidius 137
Memoria 90
μέν = quidem 100
μέντοι following δέ 178
Metaphors,   "dead"   73,   123 t,
   125
   from balance 116
   darkness 141
   death (*mortalis*) 146
   fires 32, 33
   military affairs 66
   physical facts 104
   waves (*sedare pugnam*) 129
   yoke 189
Mihi crede 88
Minervam sus 57
Miseria, subject to transitive verb
   166 ; *see* "Abstract"
Modal gerund of Livy = present par-
   ticiple 192
"Modern"; *see* "Haec"
Momentum 116
Mons Sacer 192
Moods ; *see* "Indicative," "Sub-
   junctive," etc.
Mortalis metaphorical 146
Mos = "bad   custom"   56,   cp.
   "Iura"
Mourning, period of 165
Movere, order of 31
   with abstract and inanimate sub-
   jects 185
Movet terra 195
Muliebris 81, 121 ; *see* "Mundus"
Mulierculae 184
Munditiae 185 b
Mundus muliebris 186
Municipia 172
"My dear Marcus," order of in
   Latin 45

Names; *see* "Proper"

Nascuntur)(natae sunt 93

Navales socii, meaning of and order 158

Nē = *val* 104 b

Ne = ut ne 33

Ne feceris 108

Ne...nec = ne...neve 34
  ne...nec...neu...aut 34
  ne...ve 34

"Nearer to," how translated 36

Nec = ἀλλ᾽ οὐ 134
  followed by *aut* 185
  for *neve* 34
  necne)(annon 50
  preceded by *non* = οὐ...οὐδέ 80 t, 185
  with *nec* subdividing an original negative 38

Necesse, constructions of 117

Necne 50

Negare; *see* "Aio"

Negative brought forward in Latin 33, 34, 36, 59, 97, 144, 185
  careless position of in English 115 b, 116 t (cp. 136)
  repeated as a connective 82 b
  statement of English = question in Latin 66, 151 b, 165

"Neglected to," how translated 48 t

Neuter adjective = noun 58, 76, 97, 118 b, 121, 126, 132, 134, 142 t, 161, 195
  adjective or pronoun to express specific word of English 64, 68 (bis), 79, 85 t, 104, 111, 112, 119, 138, 146, 147, 148, 150 t, 167, 168, 184, 185
  pronoun combined with *res* 109
  with gender ambiguous 67, 109
  with nouns of different gender 97 t, 186

Neve, followed by *aut* 34
  followed by *ve* 34
  preceded by *ne* 34

"Newcastle, Coals to" 58 t

"No," translated by adversative asyndeton 69

Noli facere 108

Nomen = gens 181

Non = "and not," "but not" 119, 183, 191

Non brought forward for emphasis, 158 t
  position of 102
  non...nec...nec = οὐ...οὐδέ...οὐδέ 80 t, 185
  non...solum, with emphatic word between 115

Nonne, position of 128, 130, 131, 133 t

Nostra, etc. as antecedent to relative 50
  with *interest* 50

Nostri -um 45

Noun of English > Verb of Latin; *see* "Verb"
  of English represented by neuter adjective; *see* "Neuter Adjective"
  of Latin > Verb of English 128

Novus)(antiquus 70
  position of 133
  with bad meaning 70, 125, 134, 152

Nulla feminine of *nemo* 91, 180 t

Nullus = *non* 92
  followed by *nc...quidem* 38, 61
  subdivided by *aut...aut* or *nec... nec* 38

Nunc = νῦν δέ 46 b, 47 t, 114 b

Object; *see also* ORDER, and "Subject"
  brought forward becomes subject; *see* "Subject"
  or equivalent and subject put early 77 t, 84
  supplied readily 67, 68, 89, 91, 180 t
  translated by "is the object of" 70, 84

Oblata; *see* "Data"

Oblique Narration, Indicative in 143

Occupatus ± *in* 162 b

Offundere 141

ὀλιγωρεῖν 104

Omission of copula with *quo...eo* 85
  of *esse* 109 t; *see* "Esse"
  of preposition with *totus, cunctus*, etc. 128 t

Omnis without preposition *in* 128 t
  with sense of παντοῖος 86

"One" = tibi 98

"On foot" = pedibus 182

"Open a book" = evolvere 126

Oportet = "would be right" 105

Oppia Lex 152

Oppian Law, order of adjective 30, 163

Oppidum)(urbs 35

Oratio Obliqua, Indicative in 143 praeparata...accuratior 117 t

Orbitas, subject to transitive verb 190; see "Abstract"

ORDER; see also "Antecedent," "Anticipatory," "Comple-ment," "Genitive," "Object," "Relative," "Subject"

    Ablative preceding subject = sub-ject 72, 73, 128

    Abnormal order to express after-thought 94, 106 b, 131 t, 143 for exclamatory effect 42, 79 (cp. 115), 89, 155

    Adjective after verb 124 (bis) of number and quantity 27, 123, 129, 160 b, 165, 196 prepositive or separated 46, 59 b, 63, 73, 81, 83, 87, 88, 89, 90, 92, 95, 107, 110, 119, 126, 127, 132 t, 134, 137, 138 t, 143, 148 t, 149, 153, 162, 169, 170, 176, 179, 188 (bis), 190, 191, 197

    Adverb or equivalent preceding subject 47, 64, 91, 188, 189 t postpositive 81, 96, 110, 113, 120 t, 140 t separated from verb 65, 69, 96, 107, 121, 158 t

    Aliquis postpositive 143, 145 (bis)

    ἀπὸ κοινοῦ 56, 68, 76, 95, 97, 145, 192 (bis)

    Chiasmus 56, 82, 89, 118, 143, 162, 167 b

    Demonstrative between interroga-tive and noun 56

    Final Clause 133 b

    Genitive partitive separated 45, 46, 142 prepositive 36, 48, 53, 55, 65, 83, 89, 90, 91, 137, 138, 164, 166, 171, 175, 180, 183, 184 t, 186, 196 (bis) separated for emphasis 56

ORDER

    Gist of construction early 57, 77 t, 84, 89, 137

    Movere comes early 31

    Object brought forward 36, 54, 59, 72, 101, 102 t, 105

    Oppia Lex 30, 163

    Participle prepositive 130, 131, 181, 192, 193, 197

    Partitive genitive; see Genitive above

    Phrase constructionally complete must be complete in sense 86, 89, 110, 122, 125 t, 131 t, 136, 152, 159, 164, 168

    Phrase following verb 86, 88 b, 89

    Phrase preceding subject = subject 97, 129, 132, 163, 166, 170, 171, 183, 190

    Subject; see also "Subject" early in Latin)(English 38 last for emphasis 186 preceding *cum* clause but not subject to principal clause also 148, 194

    Verb early for emphasis 116 of saying, showing, etc. comes early 37, 69, 124 t, 142, 146, 179

    Verb, object, subject 31

    Word contrasted comes early 75, 76 t, 106, 168 emphatic comes early 65, 69 t, 109 t, 153, 159, 163, 165, 178, 181, 182, 191 emphatic lies between adverb and conjunction 115, 124 b, 173, 177 single or phrase coming after verb, especially an iambus 59, 67, 75, 76, 80, 87, 133, 137 b, 145 b, 156 b, 169, 173, 174, 191

"Origines" of Cato 126

Ornament of English)(Latin sim-plicity 38, 52 b, 104, 114, 166, 183

"Ornate Alias" 46, 119, 125

Ornatus 185 b, 186 t

ὅσιος 82 t

"Otherwise," how translated 130

οὐ...οὐδέ...οὐδέ=non...nec...nec 80 t, 185

"Over, to triumph" = triumphare de... 82

Panoramic; see "Imperfect"

παντοῖος represented by πᾶς and omnis 86

Par est 105

παρά = per 122

παραιτητός 107 b

Parallelism; see "Formality," "Preciseness," "Variety" 35; varied by Chiasmus 57 t

παρελθεῖν = procedere 113

Parenthetic phrases 91 b

Participle of English)(new principal verb of Latin 68, 76, 191
  +ut, utpote, velut, quasi, tamquam, etc. 82
  separated from auxiliary 140 b
  translates abstract noun 156 t, cp. "Gerundive"

Partem in bonam accipere 113 t

Partitive; see "Genitive" and ORDER

Parva, subject to transitive verb 185

πᾶς = παντοῖος 86

Passive avoided by subjunctive of Ideal 2nd person 49

Paterfamilias 45, 175

Patres)(Quirites and order of 44, 103

Patria)(civitas, respublica 77

Paupertas 100, 102

Pax, subject to transitive verb 147

Pecunia, plural of 161, 166, 168; see "Praesens"

πείθειν χρήμασι, δώροις 91

Per = παρά 122
  to express agent 90 b

Perfect; see Appendix B, and "Subordinate Clause"
  Aorist in consecutive clauses 163 b, 164, 165
  Aorist Indicative with cum 78
)(Imperfect 92 b
)(Present 93
  Historical 153
  instead of Imperfect or Pluperfect 77, 78, 131, 132

Perfect Subjunctive in dependent questions 153, 154
  Subjunctive in -arint 151

Periphrastic Future, for Future where principal clause is Present 51

Pertinente; see "Ablative"

Pessimo publico 127 t

Pietas, meaning of 79
  subject to transitive verb 80

Piso, Calpurnius 192

Pius 79

Placet diis + si 62

Play on phrase inferre signa 88

"Plea," how translated 80 b

Plebi for plebis 30 t, 62 b, 112

Plebs, Secession of 192

Pleonasm "Livian" 144, 161

Plerumque, meaning of 147 t

Pluperfect Subjunctive = future perfect of Recta 167

Plus = plusquam 34 t
  internal accusative 194 t

πολύπτωτον 186

Porta)(ianua 196

Possessive adjective as antecedent; see "Nostra"

Poterat + infinitive)(potuit 184

"Pour" intransitive)(Latin 195

Praefringere 172

Praeparata oratio 117 t

Praesens pecunia 168 b, cp. "Repraesentare"

Praesentem dare, exigere, ferre 169 t

Praetexere 172

Praetextatus 171 b

Preciseness of Latin; see "Formality," "Parallelism," "Variety," 38, 43, 52, 53, 106, 142

Predicative dative 147

Preposition; see "Gerund," and "In" omitted with totus, medius, etc. 128 t
  + demonstrative of English > adverb of Latin 36 t
  with different cases and noun repeated 194 b
  with names of towns 88, 157

Prepositional phrases
  qualifying nouns 39, 40, 80, 129, 140, 141 t, 157, 170

Prepositional phrases translated by adjective of Latin 51 b
by genitive of Latin 39, 55, 65, 86, 92, 94, 97, 165, 167 t, 171 t, 173, 177, 179
Present in English becomes Latin future 75, 105, 106, 108, 111, 141, 188, 193
Present perfect)(present 93
Principio; see "A"
Priusquam with subjunctive 109
Probus 81
Procedere = παρελθεῖν 113
Profanus 82 t
Profestus 81, 82
Promulgare 113
Pronouns; see "Neuter"
different for same person 182
grouped together 57; see "Case-relations"
inserted for emphasis 49, 63, 89, 108, 111 t, 142, 191, 193
of English represented by repeated word of Latin 35, 130, 131, 134, 167, 171
supplied easily in Latin 67, 68
Proper names in plural 36; see "C"
order abnormal 129 b
Propitius, derivation of 89 b
Propius = propius quam 35
πρόρριζον 48
Publico + bono, malo, pessimo 127 t
Publicum 56, 58, 76, 97
Pudere, future perfect of 105
used personally 105
Pudor = feeling of shame 99
subject to transitive verb 59
Pueri)(liberi 108, 172
Puerilis 81, 121
Purgare, meanings of 134, 135
Purpose clause, order of 133 b

Quae; see "Relative"
Quam supplied after plus 34; after propius 35
Quamquam = καίτοι 58 b + participle 82
Quasi + participle 82
Que = "or" 37 (bis), 114 t, 195 (cp. et 190)
like ve 61 (see "Ac," "Aut," "Ve")

Que subdividing et...et 43 (cp. ve)
with last member of series 37, 108
with prepositions 67 (cp. 194)
Questions, dependent; see "Indicative," "Perfect," "Subjunctive"
indignant; see "Indicative"
of Latin = negative statement of English 66, 151 b, 165
Qui; see "Relative"
= talis ut + subjunctive 76 (bis)
+ tamen as connective 117
Quid? = "furthermore" = καὶ μήν, τί δέ; 68, 129
= "Well?" 149
Quid aliud ± facere 62, 187
Quid tandem 125
Quidam = "as it were" 54
Quidem = μέν 100, 177; see "Et quidem"
Quilibet; see "Ullus"
Quin, construction with 197
Quippe + participle 82
Quirites, meaning and order of 44, 103
Quis adjectival 141
Quisquam)(ullus 95, 139
Quisque, position of 75
)(uterque 142
"Quite" = satis 73
Quivis; see "Ullus"
Quo picked up by eo 85
Quo ne + comparative 162
Quod = cum + indicative 96 t; see "Cum"
Quod nisi 54
Quod si 54
Quoniam 179
Quoque = καί = "on the other hand," etc. 112, 114, 133, 150 b
preceded by et 62

Rationem inire 98
"Reason of," how to translate 156
Recens)(vetus 70, 149, 152
Reddere epistulam 168
Regius 87
Regnum 87
Relative, antecedent in possessive adjective 50
ambiguous forms, neuter or masculine 67
asyndeton with 147

Relative as connective 44, 50, 67, 117
  (+ *tamen*), 152
  picked up by demonstrative 71,
  75, 85 (*quo...eo*), 135, 146
  purpose expressed by 95 b, 97,
  124, 158, 169
  quo ne 162
Religio, subject to transitive verb
  80
Rĕmus 127
Repetere 132
Repetition; *see also* "Variety"
  of adjective 29, 48 (bis), 116 b,
  168
  of negatives as connective 82 b
  of noun 35, 38 t, 41 (bis), 42, 43,
  46, 58 (bis), 63, 73, 119, 120 b,
  121, 123, 125, 126, 130 (bis), 131,
  133 (bis), 134, 136, 140, 141,
  144, 146, 164 b, 167, 168 t,
  169, 171, 173, 194 (with different
  prepositions)
  of noun in Latin for pronoun
  of English 35, 130, 131, 134,
  167, 171
  of phrase as connective 83, 182 t
  of preposition 82 (as connective),
  178
  of verb 103, 107, 108, 124, 135 b,
  139 b, 151, 167 (bis), 169, 172,
  173, 176, 188, 191, 194
  of verb as connective 30
  in answering questions 92
Repraesentare pecuniam 168 b, cp.
  "Praesens"
Res as subject to transitive verb
  87 b
  combined with neuter pronoun
  109
  = episode 27, struggle 31, story
  48, proposal 49, weal 50, business 61, acquisitions 87, matter
  92, position 109, measure 119,
  evidence 120, exaggeration 124,
  fortunes 133, conditions 136,
  objection 142, example 161
Resolved forms of subjunctive
  have auxiliary in indicative 60,
  184
  when dependent 114
Resolved forms of future 193
Respublica)(civitas, patria 77

Rex 87
Rhetorical devices in Latin; *see*
  "Anaphora"
  artificial contrasts 73, 196 t
  doublets 47
Rhythm verse; *see* "Hexameter"
Rogare legem 107
Rogationem ferre 30
Rōmulus 127
"Root and branch" 48
Rudem gladiator 58 t

Sacer Mons 192
Sagatus 171 b
Salvus = superstes 189
Sane 192
Satis = "quite" 73
Saturn, temple of 161
Saying, verbs of early; *see*
  "Showing"
Scilicet 192
Se referring to subjective genitive
  179
Secession of Plebs 192
"Secondly"; *see* "Firstly"
Sed; *see* "Asyndeton" and "Vero"
  word of positive meaning supplied
  after 70, 71
Sed...etiam, word of interest be-
  tween 115, 124 b
Sedare pugnam, etc. 129
Seeing, verbs of come early; *see*
  "Showing"
"Seems that, It"; *see* "It"
Sententiam in eandem 112 b
Separation of auxiliary from par-
  ticiple 140
  of partitive genitive 46, 142
Servulus 184
Severus 141
"Shame, feeling of" 99
Showing, verbs of early 37, 69,
  124 t, 142, 146, 179
Si = num;...nĕ 74
  preceded by anticipatory *ita* 90
Si diis placet, meaning of 62
Sicut 169, 179
Signa inferre, play on 88
Signatum aurum 162
Simile formally expressed in Latin
)(English 147
Simplicity of Latin; *see* "Ornament"

Simul = *simul ac* 69, 104 b, 108
  picked up by *extemplo* 69
Sin 54
Sin minus 54
Socii Latini nominis 181
Socii navales, meaning and order
  of 158
Soleatus 171 b
Sollicitudo, subject to transitive
  verb 80
Spes nostra = "our hope*s*" 47
Sponta + sua 52, 119
Statement, negative of English >
  question of Latin 66, 151 b, 165
Status subject to transitive verb 145
Stragula vestis 175
Stronger expressions in Latin 117 b,
  cp. 115 t
Sua + *interest*)(*ipsius* 50, 51
  + *sponte*, 52, 119
Suadere legem, etc. 37, 62, 113 b,
  118
Subject, absence of with *aiebat* 179;
  see "Inquit"
  expressed by ablative preceding
    the subject 72, 73, 128, 130, 131
  by genitive prepositive 90, 166,
    171
  by object or the like brought
    early 54, 55, 59, 171, 180
  by phrase preceding subject 97,
    129, 163, 170, 183, 190
  logical; *see* ORDER throughout
  preceding subordinate clause
    though not subject to principal
    clause 148, 194
Subjective; *see* "Genitive"
Subjunctive; *see* "Apodosis," "Indicative," and "Resolved Forms"
  Attracted 98
  Concessive with *ut* 98
  Consecutive; *see* "Perfect"
  double work of 114
  = indicative of auxiliary + infini-
    tive 60, cp. 184
  Imperfect)(Pluperfect 45, 46, 97,
    110
  Imperfect where English has
    present 60
  Jussive dependent 33 b, 93 t, 159 t,
    162 t
  of English 106

Subjunctive of Ideal 2nd person 49
  of "non-fact" 183
  of reported reason 121
  perfect aorist in consecutive clause
    163 b, 164, 165
  perfect in *-arint* 151
  perfect in dependent questions 153,
    154
  pluperfect = future perfect of Recta
    167
  Potential 111
  with *antequam*, *priusquam* 109
Subordinate Clause; *see also* "Perfect"
  past consecution in Cicero and
    Livy 93, 163 b, 164, 165
  tense of, fixed by tense of principal
    clause 51, 75, 90, 105, 106, 108,
    111, 141, 143, 153, 183, 187, 188,
    193
Superbae aures 137
Superlative of exaggeration 115 t
Supine so-called 28, 81
Sus Minervam 57
Suus, order of with *sponte* 52, 119
  order of with *quisque* 45
  place of taken by *is* 77
  referring to the object of verb
    59 b, 90

Tacitus 116
Talis; *see* "Hic," and "Is"
Tamen, order of 91
  + *qui* 117
Tamquam + participle 82
  + subjunctive 183
Tandem; *see* "Quid"
  with interrogative 125, 148, 154
Tantum = solum 170, cp. 173 b
τελευτᾶν ἐς 29
Temple of Saturn 161
Tempus = καιρός 143, 168
  meaning of plural 122
  subject to transitive verb 145, 156 b
Tenacitas 177
Tense; *see* "Subordinate Clause"
θεραπεύειν τὸ ναυτικόν 158
"The" as instrumental case 85
"The" = *is*, *ille* 130
"Therefore"; *see* "And therefore"
Thinking, verbs of early; *see*
  "Showing"

τί γάρ; 68
Tibi = τινι 98
Time, expressions of indefinite in
    Latin 54
    duration of expressed by ablative
    144
Togatus 171 b
Tot separated from noun 153
Totus without *in* 128 t
Towns with preposition 88, 157
"Triumph over" = triumphare de 82
Tu; *see* "Tibi"
    inserted for emphasis 108
Tueri classem 158
Tum picking up *cum* 113
Tunicatus 171 b
Turba = "crowds" 37;)(agmen 54

Ullus + *alius* 95
)(*quisquam, quivis, quilibet* 95,
    139
Ultro 96
Universus 75, 133, 180
ὑπάρχειν 179 t
Urbs)(oppidum 35
Usus subject to transitive verb 144 b,
    145 t, 160
Ut...ita, expressed by *et...et* 109
    Consecutive usually preceded by
    anticipatory *ita, adeo,* etc. 163 t;
    see also "Perfect"
    Explanatory 33
    "Granting that," picked up by
    sic 98
    limiting 120
    + participle 82
    preceded immediately by *ita* 158 b,
    159
    repeated after a lengthy clause
    72 t
Uter)(*quis* 148
Uterque)(*quisque* 142
Uti, utilis in aliquid 175
Utpote + participle 82
Utrum omitted 53 t
Utrumque)(utraque 101 t

Variety; *see* "Repetition"
    "Livian" 66, 67, 93, 123 t
    of English 38, 43, 44, 52, 53,
    83 (bis), 108, 150, 151 t, 182 b,
    197 t

Variety,   contrast   Latin   which
    (*a*) repeats previous verb (*see*
    "Repetition"), (*b*) supplies
    previous verb 33, 34, 53, 61,
    73, 82, 93, 181, (*c*) waits for
    verb 62, 68, 74, 116, 191
    English has present participle;
    Latin continues with fresh verb
    68, 76, 191
    reason for variety 38
Ve, expressing minor alternative 35,
    cp. "Vel"
    like *que* = "or" 61
    preceded by *ne* 34
    see "Ac," "Aut," "Que"
Vectare)(vehere 82
Vehiculo; *see* "Iuncto"
Vel...vel)(aut...aut 64
    subdivides *aut* 35
Velim 111
Velut + participle 82
Verb of Latin > noun of English 37,
    41, 44, 50, 52, 58, 67, 68 b, 70,
    73 (bis), 80 (bis), 82, 84, 85, 89,
    91, 103, 104, 111, 112, 117 b, 118,
    122, 124, 127 (bis), 129, 131, 136 b,
    138 t, 139, 140, 148 b, 149, 154
    (bis), 155 b, 156 (bis), 157, 159,
    160 t, 163, 164, 167, 176, 186,
    188, 191, 194 (bis)
    of English > noun of Latin 128
    of saying, showing, believing, etc.
    comes early 37, 69, 124 t, 142,
    146, 179
    repeated in answering a question
    92
    supplied readily 93, 181; *see*
    "Variety"
Verba magna 123
Vere dicere 65
Verecundia, subject of transitive
    verb 54, 55
Vero following *sed* 178
Verse rhythm; *see* "Hexameter"
Vestis stragula 175
Vestra antecedent to relative 50
    with *interest* 50
Vestri -um 45, 100
Vetus 70, 149, 154 b
Vexation, feeling of 99
"Vicarious" *facere* 169
Videre = ἐφορᾶν 181

Videres 111 b

Videri personal in Latin)(English 103, 157

Viduae, meaning of 132 b, 161

Viduitas, subject to transitive verb 190

Vir)(homo 115 t

Virilis 81, 121

Vos inserted for emphasis 111 t

Weaker expressions in English, 117 b, cp. 115 t

"Well" = *quid?* 149

"Without doing," how translated 120

For EU product safety concerns, contact us at Calle de José Abascal, 56–1°,
28003 Madrid, Spain or eugpsr@cambridge.org.

www.ingramcontent.com/pod-product-compliance
Ingram Content Group UK Ltd.
Pitfield, Milton Keynes, MK11 3LW, UK
UKHW012328130625
459647UK00009B/136